CLICKS TO CASH
76 WAYS TO MAKE MONEY ONLINE WITH NO REAL SKILL

BY ELMA D. WISCONSIN

Copyright © 2024 | Elma Wisconsin
All rights reserved.

This Book is Dedicated to
my Incomplete Love.

INTRODUCTION

WELCOME TO THE WORLD OF ONLINE INCOME!

Imagine this: you wake up, grab your coffee, check your phone, and see notifications that you have made money—while you were sleeping! This is not a fantasy. For millions around the world, making money online has become a way of life. Whether you are looking for a side hustle, a way to make a little extra cash, or even a full-time income, the internet is the gold mine just waiting to be tapped into.

In 2023, an estimated **3.5 billion people**—almost half of the world's population—engaged in some form of online commerce or digital work. The beauty of making money online is that it is accessible to anyone, anywhere, with an internet connection. No longer is it just for the highly skilled, the tech-savvy, or the entrepreneurs with capital. It is for you. If you have the motivation, there is a way for you to start earning right now, regardless of your current experience or skill set.

WHAT YOU CAN EXPECT FROM THIS BOOK

The truth is, making money online will not always be a "get rich quick" scenario. It takes some time, a bit of effort, and a willingness to learn. But it is not challenging work in the traditional sense. You will not be sweating away on an assembly line or clocking in for long hours at a retail store. Instead, you will be clicking, uploading, typing, and sharing. Sounds a bit easier.

In this book, you will find **seventy-six of the easiest ways** to make money online—none of which requires exceptional skills or training. You can do them with the tools you already have, whether that is your phone, tablet, or laptop. Whether you are interested in quick cash or want to set up streams of passive income, you will find options here that fit into your schedule, suit your lifestyle, and align with your goals.

WHY NOW IS THE BEST TIME TO START

As the world becomes more connected, the opportunities to make money online are exploding. According to *Statista*, the global e-commerce market was worth over **$5.7 trillion** in 2022, and it is projected to grow by at least 10% each year. This is not just a statistic; it's an indicator of how people are increasingly willing to spend, sell, and share online. That's where you come in.

The demand for online services is higher than ever, and more companies and individuals are outsourcing work, seeking fresh content, and looking for innovative products. Platforms like Fiverr, Etsy, and YouTube have allowed people to earn money simply by sharing their hobbies, skills, or even their personalities. Even more accessible are the platforms that allow you to get paid for easy tasks like watching videos, taking surveys, or giving feedback on websites. Are opportunities endless, and the best part? They're often only a few clicks away.

GETTING STARTED: TOOLS AND SETUP ESSENTIALS

You don't need a fancy office or a professional-grade setup to get started. Here's a list of the basic tools that will help you make the most of the strategies in this book:

1. **A Reliable Internet Connection**: This one's a no-brainer. A strong, reliable internet connection will be your gateway to a world of income opportunities. Most tasks don't require high-speed fiber, but the better your connection, the more smoothly you can work.

2. **A Device (Laptop, Tablet, or Smartphone)**: Depending on the type of work you're interested in, you'll need a device with internet access. While a smartphone is more than enough for many tasks, a laptop or tablet will broaden your options and allow you to do more in less time.

3. **Basic Software and Apps**: For most tasks, a simple web browser will do the trick, but you might also want to have some essential apps and software on hand. For example:

    - **Google Workspace** or **Microsoft Office** for documents and spreadsheets.
    - **PayPal** or other digital payment apps to receive your earnings.
    - **Social Media Apps** for activities like content creation and promotion.

4. **A Payment Account**: Sign up for a payment service like PayPal, Venmo, or Payoneer, depending on the methods accepted by the platforms you will use. Most of these services are free to set up and will allow you to get paid quickly and easily.

5. **An Email Account**: Your email will be the command center for most of your online endeavors. Make sure it is secure and consider setting up a new email specifically for your online money-making activities to keep things organized and professional.

6. **Optional: A Camera or Microphone**: If you are interested in opportunities like YouTube, podcasting, or streaming, investing in a decent camera or microphone can pay off. But do not worry, even if you don't have these, plenty of options in this book won't require them.

With these basic tools, you'll be ready to dive into the methods outlined in the coming chapters. Remember, you don't need everything at once. You can start small, with what you have, and build your toolkit over time as you explore different methods.

SETTING YOURSELF UP FOR SUCCESS

The methods in this book are beginner-friendly, but that doesn't mean you should dive in without a plan. Here are a few tips to help you maximize your online earnings:

- **Set Small, Achievable Goals**: Whether it's making $50 this month or trying three new methods from the book, setting goals will keep you motivated and make the process more rewarding.

- **Experiment and Explore**: Don't feel limited to just one method. Try a few to see which ones you enjoy, and which ones bring the most return. You might be surprised by what you find fulfilling!

- **Stay Organized**: Track your earnings, especially if you're trying multiple methods. A simple spreadsheet can help you see where your time is best spent.

- **Have Patience and Consistency**: The online money-making journey is different for everyone. Some methods might take time to show results, but if you stick with them, you'll see the rewards.

So, let's get started! The possibilities are out there, just waiting for you to take advantage of them. Whether you're a student, a stay-at-home parent, or someone looking to supplement your income, these strategies are designed to fit your lifestyle. Let's dive in and transform your clicks into cash!

CHAPTER 1:
QUICK CASH – FAST AND SIMPLE WAYS

If you're eager to start making money online but don't want to dive into anything too time-consuming or complex, this chapter is for you. Here, you'll find simple ways to earn a little extra cash with minimal effort. These methods won't make you rich, but they're perfect for quick wins that you can do in your free time. Let's dive into 12 of the easiest ways to start earning right away!

1. TAKING ONLINE SURVEYS

Online surveys offer a straightforward way to earn money without any special skills. Companies and brands are eager to get real consumer feedback to shape their products, services, and marketing strategies. This need translates into millions of surveys posted online every month, giving you a chance to share your thoughts on a variety of topics while getting paid for it.

- **How It Works**: Survey sites partner with companies seeking consumer feedback. When you sign up on these platforms, you'll be asked to fill out a profile survey to help match you with relevant surveys. Once matched, you'll receive survey invitations via email or directly on the platform. Surveys can vary in length, from 5 minutes to half an hour, and in complexity. Most platforms pay either in cash, points (redeemable for cash), or gift cards.

- **Earnings Potential**:
    - The earnings from surveys can range significantly. A quick, 5-minute survey might earn you $0.50, while longer, more specialized surveys can pay as much as $10-$50. According to Swagbucks, resolute users can earn between $20 and $100 per month by completing surveys and other small tasks.
    - **Pro Tip**: Stick to reputable sites like Swagbucks, Survey Junkie, and Pinecone Research to avoid scams. Avoid sites that ask for a fee to join, as most legitimate survey platforms are free.

- **Platforms to Try**:
    - **Swagbucks**: This popular platform lets you earn points (or "SB") for a range of activities, including surveys, watching videos, shopping, and playing games. You can redeem your points for gift cards from major retailers or get cash via PayPal. Swagbucks also has a browser extension that allows you to earn while you search online.

- **Survey Junkie**: Survey Junkie is one of the most user-friendly platforms. Once you reach 500 points ($5), you can redeem them for cash via PayPal or e-gift cards. They also have a browser extension that you can use to maximize earnings with minimal effort.
- **Pinecone Research**: Pinecone Research is known for its higher-paying surveys, but it's an invite-only site. If you can join, expect $3 per survey, and occasionally you'll be asked to test new products and keep them as a bonus.

- **Realistic Expectations**: While online surveys are easy, they won't replace a full-time income. Treat them as a fun way to make extra money on the side. Surveys work best for filling small gaps in your day—waiting in line, during your commute, or winding down in the evening. With steady participation, you might earn $30-$100 monthly.

2. TESTING WEBSITES AND APPS

Getting paid to test websites and apps is an excellent choice for those who enjoy exploring digital products. Companies need real people to navigate their sites or apps to find usability issues and gather feedback on user experience. If you have a reliable internet connection, a computer, or even a smartphone, you're good to go.

- **How It Works**: Website testing is typically conducted on platforms that connect testers with companies. You will be given a website or app to navigate and specific tasks to perform, such as finding a product, going through the checkout process, or exploring features. You'll also record your screen and voice as you share your thoughts aloud, providing real-time feedback.

For most tests, you'll need to describe your experience, pointing out anything confusing, enjoyable, or frustrating. Companies pay for this feedback to improve their digital products. Some tests even include added questions, written feedback, or a short interview at the end.

- **Earnings Potential**:
  - UserTesting, a popular platform, pays $10 for each 20-minute test. More in-depth interviews can pay up to $60. TryMyUI offers similar rates, typically around $10 for a 15–20-minute test.
  - **Pro Tip**: Testers with a clear speaking voice and analytical mindset often earn higher ratings and receive more testing opportunities. Also, stay logged

into your testing platforms to be among the first to grab new tests.

- **Platforms to Try**:
    - **UserTesting**: This platform offers one of the best testing rates. You'll earn $10 per 20-minute test, where you speak your thoughts aloud as you explore a website or app. You can also qualify for high-paying interviews that offer up to $60 per session. All payments are made via PayPal within seven days.
    - **TryMyUI**: Similar to UserTesting, TryMyUI pays $10 per 15-20 minute test. The platform offers tests often, and you'll need to complete a sample test to qualify. Payments are made every Friday via PayPal.
    - **Userlytics**: This platform is known for a variety of tests, from websites to mobile apps, with payment ranging from $5 to $90, depending on the complexity and duration. They offer international opportunities as well, making it accessible to testers worldwide.
- **Realistic Expectations**: Website testing can be competitive, with tests sometimes going fast once they're posted. If you're diligent, you could earn anywhere from $30 to $100 a week, depending on the number of available tests. The key is to stay active on multiple platforms and grab tests as soon as they appear. For those in popular testing countries like the US, UK, and Canada, there are generally more opportunities available.

3. WATCHING ADS AND VIDEOS FOR CASH

Imagine earning a few dollars just for watching videos or ads. It may sound too good to be true, but many platforms offer this choice as a way to make money on the side. The tasks are straightforward: watch a video, rate it, or answer a couple of quick questions afterward. It's a low-effort, passive way to earn cash while multitasking or relaxing.

- **How It Works**: Sign up on a platform that offers paid video watching opportunities. Most platforms have a variety of videos, including advertisements, movie trailers, and promotional clips. For each video you watch, you'll earn a small amount of cash or points that can be redeemed for rewards like gift cards or direct cash deposits. Some platforms also offer bonuses for watching a certain number of videos in a day.
- **Earnings Potential**:
    - Watching ads and videos is a lower-paying activity, with earnings ranging from $0.01 to $0.10 per video.

However, you can earn $20-$30 per month if you're consistent.
- ○ **Pro Tip**: Sign up for multiple platforms to maximize your earnings. Many sites also offer other activities (like surveys or cashback) that you can use to boost your earnings.

- **Platforms to Try**:
  - ○ **InboxDollars**: This site pays you to watch videos, take surveys, and read emails. Each video may only pay a few cents, but with enough volume, it can add up. Plus, inexperienced users often receive a $5 bonus just for signing up.
  - ○ **Swagbucks**: Watch videos, complete surveys, and shop online to earn "Swagbucks" (SB), which can be redeemed for gift cards or PayPal cash. Swagbucks offers a daily limit on video earnings, so it's best used as one part of your online earning strategy.
  - ○ **FusionCash**: FusionCash pays you for watching videos, among other small online tasks. They have a low payout threshold of $25, making it easier to cash out compared to some other platforms.
- **Realistic Expectations**: Watching videos is a low-effort way to earn, but don't expect to make substantial money. It's best to view this as a supplement to other online earning methods. By setting aside 10-20 minutes a day, you could potentially earn $20 or more per month. To maximize efficiency, watch videos on your phone while doing other tasks, like cooking or commuting.

4. PARTICIPATING IN PAID FOCUS GROUPS

Paid focus groups are an engaging way to provide feedback on products, services, and advertising strategies while getting compensated for your time. Companies are keen on gathering insights from consumers to refine their offerings, and they pay participants well for their opinions.

- **How It Works**: Focus groups typically involve a group of participants discussing a specific topic guided by a moderator. These sessions can take place in-person or online via video conferencing tools. Participants share their opinions, experiences, and suggestions, which can last anywhere from 1 to 3 hours.
- **Earnings Potential**:

- Compensation for focus groups can be quite lucrative, often ranging from $50 to $150 per session, depending on the length and complexity of the discussion. Some specialized studies or product tests can even pay up to $300.
  - **Pro Tip**: To maximize your earnings, take part in multiple focus groups across different platforms, and be sure to keep your profile up to date to receive more invitations.
- **Platforms to Try**:
  - **Respondent**: This platform connects researchers with participants for qualitative studies. You can filter focus groups based on your demographics, interests, and location. Payments are typically made via PayPal and can range from $50 to $300 per study.
  - **User Interviews**: Similar to Respondent, User Interviews is focused on connecting users with researchers. You can earn $50 to $150 for each interview or focus group, with opportunities available both online and in-person.
  - **FocusGroup.com**: This site specializes in focus group studies and market research, offering a range of topics and formats. They provide a straightforward registration process, and payments usually occur shortly after your participation.
- **Realistic Expectations**: While paid focus groups can offer high returns, they can also be competitive and limited in availability. Expect to join several platforms to find enough opportunities. With consistent participation, you might earn a few hundred dollars monthly, depending on how often you can fit sessions into your schedule.

5. DATA ENTRY

Data entry is a classic online job that involves inputting, updating, or keeping data in various formats, from spreadsheets to databases. It's perfect for those looking for straightforward tasks that don't require advanced skills, making it a popular choice for beginners.

- **How It Works**: Data entry jobs typically require you to work with specific software or platforms provided by the employer. You may be tasked with entering information from paper documents, updating databases, or transcribing audio recordings. Accuracy and diligence are crucial since data integrity is essential for businesses.

- **Earnings Potential**:
  - Earnings in data entry can vary significantly based on experience and the type of data entry work you take on. Entry-level positions might pay around $10 to $15 per hour, while more experienced data entry specialists can earn $20 or more per hour.
  - **Pro Tip**: To enhance your earnings, consider specializing in a niche area, such as medical transcription or legal data entry, which often command higher rates due to the ability needed.
- **Platforms to Try**:
  - **FlexJobs**: This platform specializes in remote and flexible job opportunities, including data entry. FlexJobs curates its listings to ensure quality and legitimacy, making it easier to find trustworthy positions. Membership is needed, but the investment can pay off by saving you time and effort.
  - **Upwork**: Upwork is a freelance marketplace where you can find data entry jobs from clients worldwide. Create a profile showcasing your skills and start bidding on projects that fit your expertise and interest. Rates vary widely depending on the client and project complexity.
  - **Clickworker**: Clickworker is a microtask platform where you can complete small tasks, including data entry, text creation, and categorization. Payments are made weekly, and the tasks are typically simple, making it a good choice for beginners looking to earn money on the side.
- **Realistic Expectations**: Data entry jobs can be plentiful, but they often require time and effort to secure higher-paying gigs. Depending on the availability of work and your commitment, you could earn anywhere from $200 to $1,000 monthly. Remember that building a reputation and gaining experience will help you land better-paying jobs over time.

6. SIGNING UP FOR CASHBACK APPS AND SITES

Cashback apps and websites offer an easy way to earn money back on your everyday purchases. They partner with retailers to provide consumers with a percentage of their spending returned as cash or rewards. It's like getting paid for shopping!

- **How It Works**: When you shop through cashback apps or sites, you'll earn a percentage of your purchase amount back in cash. This can apply to various categories, including groceries, clothing, electronics, and travel. You can earn cashback either by shopping through the app or by uploading receipts from in-store purchases.

- **Earnings Potential**:
    - The cashback percentage varies by retailer and category. Most cashback apps offer between 1% to 10% back, with some promotions offering even higher rates for select items or brands. Some users report earning anywhere from $10 to $50 monthly, depending on their shopping habits.
    - **Pro Tip**: Combine cashback offers with sales, promotions, and coupon codes to maximize your savings. It's also smart to check multiple apps to see which one offers the best cashback for a specific purchase.
- **Platforms to Try**:
    - **Rakuten**: Formerly known as Ebates, Rakuten is one of the most popular cashback platforms, offering a wide range of retailers and cashback opportunities. You can earn cashback by shopping through their site or using their browser extension to alert you to available cashback offers.
    - **Ibotta**: Ibotta is primarily used for grocery shopping, allowing users to earn cashback on in-store and online purchases. You simply select offers before shopping, then upload your receipt afterward to receive cashback. Bonuses for completing specific tasks or shopping in particular stores can help increase your earnings.
    - **Dosh**: Dosh is an automatic cashback app that links to your credit or debit card. When you shop at participating retailers, cashback is automatically credited to your account, requiring no added effort. Dosh also offers cash back on hotel bookings and some travel expenses.
- **Realistic Expectations**: Cashback apps are a great way to earn extra money while shopping, but they shouldn't be viewed as a primary income source. With regular shopping habits and strategic use of offers, you could earn $50 to $200 a year, or even more if you're a frequent shopper. Set a budget

for your purchases and take advantage of cashback offers when you can to maximize savings.

7. EARNING FROM PAID ONLINE RESEARCH

Paid online research offers an opportunity to take part in various studies and surveys designed to gather data on consumer behavior, opinions, and preferences. This method allows individuals to contribute to meaningful research while earning money for their time and insights.

- **How It Works**: Research companies recruit participants to complete surveys, take part in interviews, or provide feedback on products and services. Participants might need to answer questions about their purchasing habits, preferences, or opinions on specific topics. The research may be conducted through online platforms or phone interviews.

- **Earnings Potential**:
    o Depending on the complexity and length of the research, participants can earn between $1 and $100 per survey or study. Some longer studies, particularly qualitative ones, may offer compensation in the $50 to $300 range.
    o **Pro Tip**: To maximize earnings, sign up for multiple research platforms and take part in as many studies as you can. Look for specialized studies that target your demographics for potentially higher payouts.

- **Platforms to Try**:
    o **Prolific**: Prolific connects researchers with participants for academic studies. The platform focuses on high-quality research, and participants can earn between $6 to $12 per hour, with payment made directly to your PayPal account.
    o **Survey Junkie**: This site offers cash or gift card rewards for completing surveys. While individual survey payouts can be small (usually between $0.50 to $3), it's easy to accumulate rewards over time by participating regularly.
    o **UserTesting**: This platform pays participants to evaluate websites and apps, providing feedback on usability and user experience. Payments range from $10 to $60 per test, depending on the study length and complexity.

- **Realistic Expectations**: Earning potential in paid online research can be variable, depending on your demographics and the number of studies available. With consistent participation, you could earn anywhere from $100 to $500 a month. Remember that some research opportunities may fill up quickly, so act fast when you find a suitable study.

8. JOINING "GET PAID TO" (GPT) SITES

Get Paid To (GPT) sites are platforms that offer users the chance to earn money or rewards by completing a variety of tasks, including surveys, watching videos, playing games, and shopping online. These sites are popular for their flexibility and ease of use.

- **How It Works**: Users sign up for GPT sites and earn points or cash for completing different activities. The tasks can range from taking surveys to testing products, watching promotional videos, or referring to friends. Each completed task earns you points, which can later be redeemed for cash or gift cards.

- **Earnings Potential**:
  - Earnings on GPT sites can vary significantly based on the type and number of tasks you complete. Many users report earning anywhere from $10 to $100 per month. However, some individuals have managed to earn over $500 monthly by investing more time and strategically completing high-reward tasks.
  - **Pro Tip**: Focus on completing tasks that offer the highest rewards for your time, such as surveys that pay more per minute or promotional offers with bonus points.

- **Platforms to Try**:
  - **Swagbucks**: One of the most popular GPT sites, Swagbucks offers users various ways to earn, including surveys, shopping, and watching videos. Users can earn SB points that can be redeemed for cash or gift cards. Sign-up bonuses and promotions make it easy to start earning quickly.
  - **InboxDollars**: InboxDollars pays users for completing surveys, watching videos, and reading emails. Unlike other GPT sites, InboxDollars offers cash payments rather than points, making it straightforward to see your earnings. New users receive a $5 bonus for signing up.
  - **MyPoints**: Like Swagbucks, MyPoints allows users to earn points by shopping online, taking surveys, and watching videos. Points can be redeemed for gift

cards or PayPal cash, and inexperienced users often receive bonuses for signing up.

- **Realistic Expectations**: While GPT sites can be fun and easy to use, the payouts are often small for each task. By consistently taking part and exploring various tasks, you could realistically earn $50 to $200 per month. Keep in mind that while you can accumulate earnings quickly, they may not provide a substantial side income without dedicating considerable time.

9. SELLING UNUSED INTERNET BANDWIDTH

Selling unused internet bandwidth is a unique way to monetize your internet connection by sharing your excess bandwidth with those who need it. This method allows you to earn passive income without much effort on your part.

- **How It Works**: When you sell your unused bandwidth, you allow other users or businesses to access your internet connection in exchange for payment. This can be particularly useful for people in areas with limited internet access. Services that ease this process often require users to install a simple application that manages the bandwidth-sharing process.

- **Earnings Potential**:
    o Earnings can vary widely based on your internet speed and how much bandwidth you are willing to share. Users typically earn between $5 to $50 monthly, with some reports of higher earnings from users with particularly fast connections.
    o **Pro Tip**: Check your internet service agreement to ensure that sharing bandwidth does not violate any terms. Some providers might impose restrictions on sharing your connection.

- **Platforms to Try**:
    o **Honeygain**: This app allows you to share your unused internet bandwidth and earn money in return. The app runs in the background, and you can earn between $1 to $3 for every 10 GB of shared bandwidth, with payouts made via PayPal or cryptocurrency.
    o **PacketStream**: Like Honeygain, PacketStream allows users to share their internet connection and earn money based on the amount of data they share. Users earn a percentage of the fees paid by customers

who use their bandwidth, and payouts can occur weekly.
    - **Mysterium Network**: This platform connects users who need secure and anonymous internet access with those willing to share their connection. Participants can earn cryptocurrency for sharing bandwidth, making it a unique option for tech-savvy users.
- **Realistic Expectations**: Selling unused internet bandwidth is a passive income source that can generate some extra cash each month. However, it may not be a significant income stream unless you have a fast and stable internet connection. With consistent sharing, you might earn anywhere from $10 to $100 monthly, depending on demand and your bandwidth capacity.

10. SELLING UNUSED GIFT CARDS

Unused gift cards can be a hidden source of income. Many people receive gift cards they will never use, and instead of letting them gather dust, you can sell them for cash or store credit.

- **How It Works**: You can sell gift cards from retailers, restaurants, or online stores that you don't plan to use. Depending on the platform, you can sell them for cash, or trade them for gift cards from other stores you prefer. Some platforms allow users to list their gift cards for sale at a discount.
- **Earnings Potential**:
    - The value of sold gift cards generally ranges from 60% to 90% of their face value, depending on demand and the retailer. For example, if you have a $100 gift card, you might sell it for $70 to $90.
    - **Pro Tip**: Check multiple platforms to find the best offer for your gift card. Timing can also affect the price—some holidays might increase demand for certain retailers.
- **Platforms to Try**:
    - **Cardpool**: Cardpool allows users to sell or trade gift cards. You can sell your card directly for cash or receive an instant quote for its value. Payments can be made via check or PayPal.
    - **Raise**: Raise is a marketplace for buying and selling gift cards. You can set your own price for your gift

card, and once sold, you receive payment through bank transfer or PayPal.
- **Gift Card Granny**: This site helps users compare prices from various gift card resale platforms. You can list your gift cards for sale and choose the best offer available.

- **Realistic Expectations**: Selling unused gift cards can provide some extra cash, especially if you have multiple cards to sell. Depending on how many you have and their value, you could earn anywhere from $50 to $300 monthly. Just keep in mind that selling gift cards often requires patience, as you may need to wait for buyers.

11. RENTING OUT ITEMS (E.G., STORAGE SPACE, TOOLS) ONLINE

If you have unused items or space lying around, renting them out can be a smart way to generate income. From tools and equipment to storage space, there are various opportunities to monetize your possessions.

- **How It Works**: You can list items for rent on specialized platforms, setting your prices and availability. Potential renters browse the listings, and once they find something they need, they can book it for a specified duration. Rental transactions are typically eased through the platform.

- **Earnings Potential**:
  - Rental prices vary widely based on the item and location. For instance, renting out tools or equipment can bring in $20 to $50 per day, while storage space can earn you $100 or more monthly.
  - **Pro Tip**: To attract more renters, ensure your items are clean, well-maintained, and photographed professionally. Offering discounts for longer rental periods can also encourage bookings.

- **Platforms to Try**:
  - **Fat Llama**: Fat Llama is a peer-to-peer rental marketplace where you can list a variety of items, from photography equipment to tools. Users can earn between $10 to $100+ per rental, depending on the item and duration.
  - **Neighbor**: Neighbor focuses specifically on renting out storage space. If you have an extra garage, basement, or shed, you can rent it out to someone

needing storage. Monthly earnings can range from $50 to $500, depending on the size and location of the space.
- ○ **ShareGrid**: If you have photography or videography equipment, ShareGrid allows you to rent it out to local creatives. You can set your rates, and typical earnings can vary based on the equipment's value.

- **Realistic Expectations**: Renting out items can provide a substantial side income, especially if you have valuable tools or storage space in high demand. Depending on your offerings and the frequency of rentals, you might earn anywhere from $100 to $1,000 monthly.

12. WATCHING TV AND GIVING FEEDBACK

Watching TV shows and movies while offering feedback can be a fun way to earn some extra cash. Companies and networks often seek viewers' opinions to improve their content and marketing strategies.

- **How It Works**: Participants watch designated shows or advertisements and then complete surveys or provide feedback on their viewing experience. This might include rating the content, discussing character development, or evaluating marketing strategies.

- **Earnings Potential**:
  - ○ Earnings can vary significantly based on the type of feedback you provide. Many participants earn between $5 to $20 per survey, with some specialized focus groups offering up to $50 for in-depth discussions.
  - ○ **Pro Tip**: Be on the lookout for opportunities that allow you to watch multiple episodes or shows in a single session, maximizing your earnings for the time spent.

- **Platforms to Try**:
  - ○ **Audience Research**: This platform connects viewers with companies looking for feedback on their shows and advertisements. Participants may complete surveys or take part in focus groups, with compensation ranging from $10 to $100, depending on the study.
  - ○ **Nielsen**: Known for its television ratings, Nielsen sometimes offers incentives to participants who share their viewing habits. By installing the Nielsen app on

your devices, you can earn points redeemable for cash or prizes.

- o **Swagbucks**: While primarily a GPT site, Swagbucks offers rewards for watching short video clips and advertisements. You can accumulate points that can be redeemed for gift cards or cash.

- **Realistic Expectations**: Watching TV for money may not replace a full-time income, but it can provide a fun and easy way to earn extra cash. Depending on the number of opportunities you find and your viewing habits, you could realistically earn anywhere from $50 to $200 a month.

CHAPTER 2:
SELL YOUR STUFF – FROM CLUTTER TO CASH

13. SELLING SECONDHAND ITEMS ON EBAY

Selling secondhand items on eBay is a well-established method for individuals to declutter their homes while earning money. eBay's vast marketplace allows you to sell anything from clothing and electronics to collectibles and furniture.

- **How It Works**: You can create listings for items you no longer need, setting your own prices or opting for auction-style sales. Once a buyer makes a purchase, you ship the item directly to them. eBay provides tools to help you manage your listings, track sales, and communicate with buyers.

- **Earnings Potential**:
    - Earnings vary based on the items you sell. Many users report selling everyday items for $10 to $50, while collectible or high-demand items can fetch $100 or more. In some cases, individuals have earned thousands from a single rare item or collection.
    - **Pro Tip**: Research similar listings to price your items competitively. High-quality photos and detailed descriptions can also attract more buyers.

- **Platforms to Try**:
    - **eBay**: The primary platform for selling secondhand items, eBay allows you to reach a global audience. Be sure to consider shipping costs when setting prices, as they can significantly affect your profit.
    - **Facebook Marketplace**: This platform allows you to sell items locally without shipping costs. You can set up a listing and communicate directly with potential buyers in your area.
    - **Mercari**: Mercari is a user-friendly app that allows you to list items quickly. It is particularly popular for selling clothing, electronics, and household goods. The platform offers an easy shipping process and competitive fees.

- **Realistic Expectations**: Selling secondhand items on eBay can be a lucrative side hustle, especially if you have a lot of items to sell. With consistent effort, you could earn anywhere from $100 to $500 monthly. The key is to continuously refresh your listings and respond to potential buyers promptly.

14. SELLING VINTAGE ITEMS ON ETSY

Etsy is a popular platform for selling handmade, vintage, and unique items. If you have a passion for vintage clothing, accessories, home decor, or collectibles, Etsy can be an excellent marketplace to showcase and sell your finds.

- **How It Works**: To sell on Etsy, you need to create an account and set up a shop. You can list your vintage items for sale, complete with descriptions and photos. Etsy takes a small fee for listing and transaction costs, making it accessible for individual sellers.

- **Earnings Potential**:
    - Earnings can vary based on the rarity and demand for your items. Vintage items can sell anywhere from $10 to $100, with unique or highly sought-after items potentially fetching $200 or more.
    - **Pro Tip**: Emphasize the story behind your vintage items in your descriptions. Items with a compelling history often attract buyers and can command higher prices.

- **Platforms to Try**:
    - **Etsy**: The main platform for selling vintage items, Etsy caters specifically to buyers looking for unique and artisanal products. Use effective SEO strategies in your listings to improve visibility.
    - **Depop**: Primarily focused on fashion, Depop allows you to sell vintage clothing and accessories. The platform is popular with younger consumers, making it a wonderful place for trendy vintage items.
    - **Facebook Marketplace**: You can also use Facebook Marketplace to sell vintage items locally. This approach cuts shipping fees and allows buyers to inspect items in person before buying.

- **Realistic Expectations**: Selling vintage items on Etsy can be a profitable venture, particularly if you have a knack for sourcing unique finds. Depending on your inventory and sales strategies, you could realistically earn anywhere from $100 to $1,000 monthly.

15. DECLUTTERING WITH APPS LIKE DECLUTTR FOR BOOKS, CDS, DVDS

Decluttering your home by selling unwanted items is not only a fantastic way to create space but can also generate extra cash. Apps like

Decluttr make it easy to sell books, CDs, DVDs, and even electronics with minimal effort.

- **How It Works**: Decluttr allows users to scan barcodes of items they wish to sell. The app provides an instant valuation, and once you accept the offer, Decluttr sends you a prepaid shipping label to send your items. Upon receipt, you receive payment directly to your bank account or via PayPal.

- **Earnings Potential**:
  - Earnings will depend on the items you sell. While individual books, CDs, or DVDs may not fetch unreasonable prices, collectively, you can earn anywhere from $10 to $100 or more. Electronics like smartphones or tablets can bring in significantly higher returns.
  - **Pro Tip**: Ensure that your items are in good condition, as this will affect the offers you receive. Cleaning items and ensuring they have no damage can maximize your profits.

- **Platforms to Try**:
  - **Decluttr**: This app specializes in buying used tech, media, and textbooks, making it simple to turn unwanted items into cash. You can also sell games and electronics.
  - **BookScouter**: If you have textbooks or other books to sell, BookScouter allows you to compare prices from various buyback vendors to get the best offer.
  - **Gazelle**: This platform specializes in electronics. If you have old phones, tablets, or laptops lying around, Gazelle offers an effortless way to sell them for cash.

- **Realistic Expectations**: While selling through Decluttr and similar apps might not make you rich, it can help you clear out clutter while generating some extra cash. Depending on the volume of items you sell, you could earn anywhere from $50 to $200 a month.

16. USING FACEBOOK MARKETPLACE

Facebook Marketplace has become a popular platform for buying and selling items locally. This user-friendly platform allows individuals to connect with potential buyers in their area without any shipping hassles.

- **How It Works**: To sell on Facebook Marketplace, you simply create a listing for the item you wish to sell. This includes uploading photos, adding a description, and setting a price. Interested buyers can message you directly to negotiate or arrange a pickup.

- **Earnings Potential**:
    - You can typically sell items for anywhere from $10 to several hundred dollars, depending on the item's condition and demand. Common items sold include furniture, electronics, clothing, and household goods.
    - **Pro Tip**: To attract more buyers, take clear, high-quality photos and provide detailed descriptions. Respond promptly to inquiries to build trust and ease sales.

- **Platforms to Try**:
    - **Facebook Marketplace**: This is the primary platform for selling locally. You can list items for free and reach a broad audience through your social network.
    - **OfferUp**: Like Facebook Marketplace, OfferUp allows users to buy and sell locally. The platform has a built-in messaging feature for communication and is particularly popular for furniture and appliances.
    - **Craigslist**: This classic classified platform stays effective for local sales. You can post listings for assorted items and negotiate directly with potential buyers.

- **Realistic Expectations**: Selling on Facebook Marketplace can yield significant returns, especially if you have high-demand items. With consistent effort, you could earn anywhere from $100 to $500 monthly, depending on your inventory and pricing strategies.

17. SELLING YOUR PHOTOS ON STOCK PHOTO SITES

If you have a talent for photography, selling your photos on stock photo websites can be a lucrative venture. Many businesses, bloggers, and marketers need high-quality images for their projects and are willing to pay for them.

- **How It Works**: You can upload your photos to stock photo platforms, where they will be available for licensing. When someone downloads your image, you earn a commission based on the sale price. The more popular your images, the more you can earn overtime.

- **Earnings Potential**:
    - Earnings can vary significantly based on the quality of your photos and their popularity. Some photographers earn a few cents per download, while others can make hundreds of dollars monthly. Experienced contributors with a strong portfolio can earn anywhere from $200 to $1,000+ per month.
    - **Pro Tip**: Focus on trending topics or themes, such as business, lifestyle, and travel. Use relevant keywords and tags to improve your images' visibility on the platform.

- **Platforms to Try**:
    - **Shutterstock**: One of the largest stock photo agencies, Shutterstock allows photographers to earn royalties based on the number of downloads. Contributors receive a percentage of the sale price, which can increase with more downloads.
    - **Adobe Stock**: This platform integrates seamlessly with Adobe Creative Cloud, making it an excellent option for photographers who use Adobe software. Contributors earn 33% of each sale.
    - **iStock**: Owned by Getty Images, iStock offers a tiered royalty structure based on exclusivity and sales volume. Contributors can earn between 15% to 45% of each sale, depending on their agreement.

- **Realistic Expectations**: Selling stock photos can be a thorough source of passive income, but it often requires time and dedication to build a large portfolio. Depending on your marketing efforts and the quality of your images, you could realistically earn anywhere from $50 to $500 a month as you set up yourself.

18. SELLING HOMEMADE CRAFTS ON ETSY

If you have a knack for crafting, Etsy provides an excellent platform to turn your creative hobbies into a source of income. From handmade jewelry and clothing to home decor and art, Etsy is known for its unique, artisanal offerings.

- **How It Works**: To sell on Etsy, you need to create an account and set up your shop. You can list your homemade crafts for sale, including detailed descriptions and high-quality photos.

Etsy charges a small listing fee and takes a percentage of each sale.

- **Earnings Potential**:
    - Earnings vary widely based on the type of crafts you sell and your pricing strategy. Many sellers earn anywhere from $10 to $100 per item, with unique or high-demand items potentially selling for much more.
    - **Pro Tip**: Engage with your audience through social media and offer limited-time promotions to attract more buyers. Consider seasonal trends to maximize your sales throughout the year.
- **Platforms to Try**:
    - **Etsy**: The premier platform for selling homemade crafts, Etsy is geared towards artists and crafters looking to highlight their work. Create a visually appealing shop with a cohesive aesthetic to attract buyers.
    - **ArtFire**: Like Etsy, ArtFire is an online marketplace for handmade items, vintage goods, and craft supplies. It caters to a niche audience and offers various tools to help you market your crafts effectively.
    - **Amazon Handmade**: This platform allows artisans to sell their handmade goods on Amazon. While it has strict guidelines, it provides access to a massive audience, potentially increasing your sales.
- **Realistic Expectations**: Selling homemade crafts on Etsy can be a rewarding venture both creatively and financially. Depending on your inventory, pricing, and marketing efforts, you could earn anywhere from $100 to $1,000 monthly.

19. FLIPPING THRIFT STORE FINDS FOR PROFIT

Flipping thrift store finds is an exciting and potentially lucrative way to make money online. It involves buying items at thrift stores, garage sales, or flea markets and reselling them for a profit.

- **How It Works**: You scout local thrift stores for undervalued items—these could include clothing, furniture, electronics, or collectibles. After buying them at a low price, you clean, repair, or upcycle them as needed before listing them for sale online.
- **Earnings Potential**:

- Many flippers report profit margins ranging from 50% to 300%, depending on the items they buy and how well they market them. A well-chosen item bought for $5 could be sold for $20 to $50 or more, especially if it is in demand.
- **Pro Tip**: Research brands and categories that are trending. Items from well-known brands or unique vintage pieces tend to sell faster and at higher prices.

- **Platforms to Try**:
  - **eBay**: A popular choice for selling thrift store finds, eBay allows you to reach a wide audience. Use auction listings for unique items and fixed-price listings for items you know the value of.
  - **Facebook Marketplace**: Great for local sales, this platform eliminates shipping costs, allowing you to sell larger items like furniture easily.
  - **Poshmark**: If you specialize in clothing, Poshmark is an excellent platform for selling thrifted apparel, especially from popular brands.
- **Realistic Expectations**: With dedication, flippers can realistically earn $200 to $1,000 monthly. Success depends on your ability to find valuable items and effectively market them.

20. SELLING DESIGNER ITEMS ON POSHMARK

Poshmark is a fashion-focused platform that allows users to sell new or gently used clothing, accessories, and shoes, particularly designer items. If you have a passion for fashion and a closet full of unused items, this could be a great avenue for you.

- **How It Works**: You create a free account on Poshmark and set up your virtual closet. List your designer items, including clear photos and descriptions, and set your prices. Poshmark takes a percentage of your sales, so factor that into your pricing.

- **Earnings Potential**:
  - Selling designer items can be quite profitable, with earnings ranging from $10 to several hundred dollars per item, depending on brand and condition. High-demand items from popular brands can lead to quick sales and higher prices.

- o **Pro Tip**: Use social media to promote your Poshmark closet. Join Poshmark parties to increase visibility and interact with other users to build a following.

- **Platforms to Try**:
  - o **Poshmark**: This is the primary platform for selling fashion items. Poshmark's community aspect allows you to network with other sellers and buyers, enhancing your sales potential.
  - o **Depop**: A favorite among younger audiences, Depop is an app-based platform where you can sell trendy, vintage, or unique fashion items. The format is like Poshmark, but it leans more toward streetwear and unique styles.
  - o **eBay**: eBay can also be used to sell designer items, particularly if you want to reach a larger audience. Make sure to highlight authenticity and include detailed descriptions.
- **Realistic Expectations**: By selling designer items on Poshmark, you could realistically earn anywhere from $100 to $1,000 monthly, depending on your inventory and pricing strategies.

21. RENTING OUT A ROOM OR APARTMENT ON AIRBNB

If you have a spare room or property, renting it out on Airbnb can be an excellent way to earn a passive income. This platform connects hosts with travelers looking for short-term lodging.

- **How It Works**: You create a listing for your space on Airbnb, including photos, descriptions, and availability. Guests can book directly through the platform. Airbnb handles payments and provides a secure system for communication.

- **Earnings Potential**:
  - o Earnings can vary significantly based on location, property type, and demand. In tourist-heavy areas, hosts can earn $100 to $300 per night. For longer stays, consider offering discounts to attract guests.
  - o **Pro Tip**: Perfect your listing with high-quality photos and detailed descriptions. Respond promptly to inquiries to increase your chances of booking.

- **Platforms to Try**:

- **Airbnb**: The leading platform for short-term rentals, Airbnb has a vast audience. Use its pricing tools to set competitive rates and track local trends.
- **Vrbo**: Like Airbnb, Vrbo focuses on vacation rentals, appealing to families and larger groups. It can be an excellent alternative if you have a whole property to rent.
- **Booking.com**: While traditionally used for hotels, Booking.com has expanded to include vacation rentals and can help you reach a different audience.

- **Realistic Expectations**: Depending on your property and location, you could realistically earn anywhere from $500 to $3,000 monthly from Airbnb rentals. Consistent hosting can lead to higher earnings, especially with positive reviews and repeat guests.

22. SELLING COLLECTIBLE ITEMS (E.G., COMICS, TRADING CARDS)

If you have a collection of comics, trading cards, or other collectibles, selling them online can be a rewarding venture. The market for collectibles is thriving, with many buyers willing to pay top dollars for rare or sought-after items.

- **How It Works**: You can list your collectibles on various platforms, providing detailed descriptions and quality images. Research market prices to set competitive prices and engage with potential buyers for negotiations.

- **Earnings Potential**:
  - Earnings can vary widely based on the rarity and demand for your items. While some common items may sell for $5 to $20, rare collectibles can fetch hundreds or even thousands of dollars.
  - **Pro Tip**: Keep your collectibles in good condition and consider professional grading for valuable items. This can significantly enhance their market value.

- **Platforms to Try**:
  - **eBay**: A popular platform for selling collectibles, eBay allows you to reach a large audience. Use auction-style listings for rare items to maximize profits.

- o **TcgPlayer**: If you have trading cards, TcgPlayer specializes in card sales and can help you connect with serious collectors.

- o **Heritage Auctions**: For high-value collectibles, consider using Heritage Auctions, which specializes in auctions for rare and valuable items.

- **Realistic Expectations**: Selling collectible items can be highly profitable, particularly if you have rare items. Depending on your collection and selling strategies, you could realistically earn anywhere from $100 to $1,000 monthly.

CHAPTER 3:
SIMPLE SERVICES – START EARNING BY HELPING OTHERS

23. VIRTUAL ASSISTANT FOR SIMPLE TASKS

Becoming a virtual assistant (VA) is a fantastic way to earn money online by helping businesses and entrepreneurs manage their administrative tasks. As a VA, you can work from anywhere and set your own hours.

- **How It Works**: Virtual assistants perform various tasks, such as managing emails, scheduling appointments, social media management, and data entry. The tasks can range from basic administrative duties to more specialized services, depending on your skills and ability.

- **Earnings Potential**:
    - Entry-level virtual assistants typically earn between $15 and $25 per hour, while experienced VAs with specialized skills can charge $50 or more per hour. Depending on your workload, monthly earnings can range from $500 to $3,000 or more.
    - **Pro Tip**: Build a niche for yourself, such as social media management or customer service, to attract specific clients and increase your earning potential.

- **Platforms to Try**:
    - **Upwork**: A freelance marketplace where you can create a profile and bid on virtual assistant jobs. This platform has a wide variety of clients looking for aid.
    - **Fiverr**: You can create service listings (gigs) for specific tasks you offer as a virtual assistant, allowing clients to hire you directly.
    - **Belay**: A company that specializes in connecting virtual assistants with businesses. They focus on providing quality VAs, making it easier to find consistent work.

- **Realistic Expectations**: As a virtual assistant, you could realistically earn anywhere from $300 to $3,000 monthly, depending on your workload and skill set. Building a solid client base can lead to more significant income over time.

24. OFFERING TRANSCRIPTION SERVICES

Transcription services involve listening to audio recordings and converting them into written text. This service is in demand across various industries, including healthcare, legal, and media.

- **How It Works**: You listen to audio files, such as interviews or lectures, and transcribe them accurately into text. Mindfulness and good listening skills are essential for this task.

- **Earnings Potential**:
    - Beginners typically earn around $15 to $30 per hour of audio transcribed. Experienced transcriptionists can earn up to $60 per hour, especially for specialized fields like medical or legal transcription.
    - **Pro Tip**: Specialize in a niche area (e.g., medical or legal transcription) to command higher rates and attract clients needing specialized skills.

- **Platforms to Try**:
    - **Rev**: This platform allows you to work as a freelance transcriptionist. You can choose the jobs you want to take on, and they pay based on the length of the audio.
    - **TranscribeMe**: Like Rev, this platform offers flexible transcription work, providing training for beginners and opportunities to increase earnings over time.
    - **Scribie**: Another transcription service where you can work on a freelance basis. Scribie allows you to select files that match your skill level and pays per audio hour transcribed.

- **Realistic Expectations**: Depending on your experience and the complexity of the audio, you could realistically earn between $200 and $1,500 monthly from transcription work.

25. BASIC TRANSLATION TASKS (FOR BILINGUALS)

If you are bilingual, offering translation services can be a lucrative way to make money online. Many businesses and individuals need documents, websites, or other content translated between languages.

- **How It Works**: You translate written content from one language to another. This can include anything from business documents to websites, marketing materials, or even subtitles for videos.

- **Earnings Potential**:

- o Translation rates vary based on the language pair and complexity of the content. On average, translators earn between $0.05 to $0.20 per word. Specialized translations (e.g., legal or technical) can earn significantly more.
- o **Pro Tip**: Focus on languages that are in high demand, such as Spanish, Mandarin, or Arabic, to maximize your earning potential.

- **Platforms to Try**:
  - o **ProZ**: A dedicated platform for translators, ProZ allows you to create a profile, highlight your skills, and bid on translation jobs posted by clients.
  - o **Gengo**: This platform connects translators with clients needing translations. You can take tests to qualify for various levels of work and set your rates.
  - o **Upwork**: As with virtual assistant work, Upwork is a great platform for freelancers. Create a profile highlighting your language skills and start bidding on translation jobs.
- **Realistic Expectations**: Depending on the volume of work and your language skills, you could realistically earn anywhere from $300 to $2,000 monthly from translation services.

26. SIMPLE GRAPHIC DESIGN ON CANVA

Graphic design does not have to be complicated, especially with user-friendly platforms like Canva. If you have a knack for creativity, you can create diverse designs for individuals and businesses.

- **How It Works**: Canva offers a drag-and-drop interface that makes it easy to design social media graphics, posters, business cards, infographics, and more. You can either sell your designs as templates or take on freelance projects for clients who need custom graphics.

- **Earnings Potential**:
  - o Depending on your experience and the complexity of the design, you can charge anywhere from $10 to $100 per project. If you sell templates, you might earn a steady income overtime as more people buy your designs.

- o **Pro Tip**: Stay updated on design trends and incorporate popular styles into your work to attract more clients.

- **Platforms to Try**:
  - o **Canva**: Start directly on Canva by creating and selling templates in their marketplace or offering design services through Canva's freelance opportunities.
  - o **Etsy**: Create and sell your graphic design templates on Etsy. Digital products are popular, and you can reach a large audience looking for unique designs.
  - o **Fiverr**: Offer specific design services, such as creating social media graphics or logos, and set your prices based on your experience and the complexity of the designs.

- **Realistic Expectations**: If you actively market your services and create a portfolio, you could realistically earn between $200 and $1,500 monthly, depending on the number of projects you take on.

27. BASIC VIDEO EDITING WITH APPS

With the rise of video content on social media and platforms like YouTube, basic video editing has become a valuable skill. If you have access to editing apps, you can start offering your services to content creators, businesses, or individuals needing video edits.

- **How It Works**: Video editing involves cutting and rearranging footage, adding transitions, music, captions, and effects to create a polished final product. Basic editing can be done on mobile apps or software like Adobe Premiere Pro, iMovie, or even online platforms like Clipchamp.

- **Earnings Potential**:
  - o Entry-level video editors typically earn between $15 and $50 per hour, while more experienced editors can charge upwards of $100 per hour or more for complex projects.
  - o **Pro Tip**: Create a showreel displaying your best work to attract clients and prove your editing skills.

- **Platforms to Try**:
  - o **Fiverr**: Create a profile to offer basic video editing services, such as cutting clips, adding effects, or

creating promotional videos. You can set your own rates based on the complexity of the work.
- o **Upwork**: Like Fiverr, you can bid on video editing projects and find clients who need your skills.
- o **YouTube**: Offer your services to content creators on YouTube. Many are looking for editors to help them produce high-quality content without spending too much time on editing.
- **Realistic Expectations**: Depending on your client base and project frequency, you could realistically earn between $300 and $2,500 monthly from video editing services.

28. OFFERING VOICEOVER SERVICES

If you have a clear speaking voice and good diction, offering voiceover services can be a rewarding way to make money online. Voiceovers are used in various projects, including commercials, audiobooks, e-learning courses, and more.

- **How It Works**: Voiceover artists record their voice reading scripts for clients. This can be done from a home studio setup with a good microphone and soundproofing. You can either charge per project or per hour of recording.

- **Earnings Potential**:
  - o Beginner voiceover artists typically earn around $20 to $100 per hour of audio, while experienced professionals can command rates of $300 or more per hour, depending on the project.
  - o **Pro Tip**: Invest in a quality microphone and audio editing software to improve the quality of your recordings, which can help you attract more clients.

- **Platforms to Try**:
  - o **Fiverr**: Offer your voiceover services with different packages based on project length or complexity. Create samples to display your voice and style.
  - o **Voices.com**: A dedicated platform for voice-over work, where you can create a profile and audition for various projects that match your voice and style.
  - o **Upwork**: Like other freelance platforms, you can create a profile and bid on voiceover projects that interest you.

- **Realistic Expectations**: Depending on your experience and the volume of work, you could realistically earn between $300 and $2,000 monthly from voiceover services.

29. CREATING RESUMES AND COVER LETTERS

If you have a knack for writing and an understanding of what employers look for, offering resume and cover letter writing services can be a profitable venture. Many job seekers struggle to present themselves effectively on paper, making your ability invaluable.

- **How It Works**: You aid clients in crafting professional resumes and tailored cover letters that highlight their skills, experiences, and qualifications. This often involves conducting interviews to gather information and understanding the job market.

- **Earnings Potential**:
    - Resume writers typically charge between $50 and $300 per resume, depending on their experience and the complexity of the client's needs. Specialized services (like executive-level resumes) can command even higher rates.
    - **Pro Tip**: Create packages that include a resume, cover letter, and LinkedIn profile optimization to provide more value and increase your earnings.

- **Platforms to Try**:
    - **Fiverr**: Offer resume writing services and create different packages based on the level of service (basic resume, full package, etc.).
    - **Upwork**: Build a profile and apply for jobs related to resume and cover letter writing. Many job seekers are looking for professionals to help them improve their application materials.
    - **LinkedIn**: Use your LinkedIn profile to display your services. Many professionals use LinkedIn to search for resume writers.

- **Realistic Expectations**: Depending on your clientele and how much you market your services, you could realistically earn between $500 and $2,000 monthly from resume and cover letter writing.

30. MANAGING SOCIAL MEDIA FOR SMALL BUSINESSES

With the ever-growing importance of social media for businesses, managing social media accounts can be a lucrative opportunity. Small businesses often struggle to keep an active and engaging online presence, which is where you come in.

- **How It Works**: As a social media manager, you create content, schedule posts, engage with followers, and analyze performance metrics for businesses. This role can include managing platforms like Facebook, Instagram, Twitter, and LinkedIn.

- **Earnings Potential**:
    - Social media managers typically earn between $15 and $75 per hour, depending on their experience and the scope of work. Monthly contracts can range from $300 to $5,000, depending on the size of the business and the services provided.
    - **Pro Tip**: Familiarize yourself with social media analytics to give valuable insights to your clients about their audience and engagement.

- **Platforms to Try**:
    - **Upwork**: Create a profile highlighting your social media skills and apply for projects posted by businesses looking for social media managers.
    - **Fiverr**: Offer specific social media management services, such as content creation, account setup, or strategy development.
    - **Hootsuite**: While Hootsuite is primarily a social media management tool, it also offers a job board where businesses post social media-related job openings.

- **Realistic Expectations**: Depending on how many clients you manage and the services you offer, you could realistically earn between $500 and $3,000 monthly as a social media manager.

31. BECOMING A MICRO-INFLUENCER ON INSTAGRAM OR TIKTOK

If you are enthusiastic about a particular niche—whether it's fashion, fitness, travel, or beauty—you can become a micro-influencer and make money by sharing your experiences and promoting products to your audience.

- **How It Works**: Micro-influencers typically have between 1,000 and 100,000 followers. Brands often partner with them for sponsored posts, affiliate marketing, or product promotions. Building an authentic and engaged following is key to attracting brand partnerships.

- **Earnings Potential**:
    - Micro-influencers can earn anywhere from $100 to $1,000 per sponsored post, depending on their niche and engagement rates. In addition to sponsored posts, affiliate marketing can provide ongoing passive income as you earn commissions on sales generated through your links.
    - **Pro Tip**: Focus on creating high-quality, authentic content that resonates with your audience to build trust and engagement.

- **Platforms to Try**:
    - **Instagram**: Use Instagram to share engaging content, connect with your audience, and attract brand partnerships. Utilize hashtags relevant to your niche to reach a broader audience.
    - **TikTok**: Create entertaining short videos that highlight your personality and interests. Brands are increasingly looking to TikTok influencers for creative marketing.
    - **Influencity**: A platform that connects influencers with brands, making it easier to find potential sponsorship opportunities.

- **Realistic Expectations**: Depending on your niche, content quality, and engagement, you could realistically earn anywhere from $200 to $3,000 monthly as a micro-influencer.

32. CLEANING UP PHOTOS USING ONLINE EDITORS

Photo editing has become an essential skill in today's digital world, especially with the rise of social media, e-commerce, and content creation. If you have an eye for detail and a bit of creativity, you can offer photo editing services to clients who need their images polished and professional.

- **How It Works**: Clients may need various photo editing services, such as removing blemishes, adjusting lighting, enhancing colors, cropping images, or even retouching to create the perfect shot. You can use online editing tools to make these adjustments without needing expensive software.

- **Earnings Potential**:

- Depending on your experience and the complexity of the edits, you can charge anywhere from $10 to $150 per photo. For bulk projects, you might offer discounts, which can help you secure larger contracts.
- **Pro Tip**: Specializing in a niche, such as wedding photography or product photos for e-commerce, can allow you to charge higher rates due to your ability.

- **Platforms to Try**:
    - **Fiverr**: Create a profile offering photo editing services. You can set different packages based on the number of photos, complexity of edits, or turnaround time.
    - **Upwork**: Build a profile and apply for freelance photo editing projects. Many businesses and individuals seek editors for specific jobs.
    - **Canva**: While primarily a design tool, Canva also has photo editing capabilities. You can offer services through Canva or use it as a platform to showcase your portfolio.
    - **Adobe Photoshop Express**: This is an online photo editing tool that allows you to enhance photos. While it requires some knowledge of Photoshop techniques, many find it user-friendly and effective.
- **Realistic Expectations**: If you actively market your services and build a client base, you could realistically earn between $300 and $2,500 monthly as a photo editor, depending on the volume of work and your pricing structure.
- **Getting Started**:
    - **Learn the Basics**: Familiarize yourself with online photo editing tools. Take advantage of tutorials available on YouTube or platforms like Skillshare to sharpen your skills.
    - **Build a Portfolio**: Before offering services, create a portfolio highlighting your editing skills. Use your photos or collaborate with friends or local businesses to prove your capabilities.
    - **Market Yourself**: Use social media platforms, such as Instagram and Facebook, to display your work and attract clients. Join photography or business groups where you can promote your services.
    - **Provide Excellent Customer Service**: Communicate clearly with clients, meet deadlines, and be open to

feedback. Satisfied clients are more likely to refer you to others or return for added work.

CHAPTER 4:
CONTENT CREATION – SHARE AND EARN

33. STARTING A YOUTUBE CHANNEL

Creating a YouTube channel can be a fun and profitable way to share your passions, knowledge, or creativity with the world. With over two billion logged-in monthly users, YouTube offers a vast audience for aspiring content creators.

- **How It Works**: You create and upload videos on topics you are enthusiastic about or knowledgeable in, such as gaming, beauty, tech reviews, education, or cooking. Once you reach specific criteria, you can monetize your channel through ads, sponsorships, merchandise, and memberships.

- **Earnings Potential**:
    - Once you qualify for the YouTube Partner Program, you can earn about $1 to $3 per 1,000 views through ad revenue. Depending on your niche, some channels make significantly more through sponsored content and affiliate marketing.
    - **Pro Tip**: Engaging content that resonates with your audience can lead to higher view counts and better ad revenue. Collaborating with other creators can also help you reach new viewers.

- **Platforms to Use**:
    - **YouTube**: Obviously, this is the primary platform for video uploads. Invest in good quality video equipment (camera, microphone) for better production value.
    - **TubeBuddy**: A browser extension that helps with keyword research, perfecting video titles, and managing your channel effectively.
    - **Canva**: Use this for creating eye-catching thumbnails and channel art.

- **Realistic Expectations**: With consistent effort and quality content, you could realistically earn between $100 to $10,000 monthly, depending on your niche, audience size, and monetization strategies.

- **Getting Started**:

- o **Choose a Niche**: Select a topic that interests you and has a potential audience. Research what other channels are doing in that space.
- o **Create High-Quality Content**: Invest time in planning, filming, and editing your videos. Aim for engaging and informative content.
- o **Perfect for SEO**: Use relevant keywords in your titles, descriptions, and tags to help your videos rank in search results.
- o **Promote Your Channel**: Share your videos on social media and engage with your audience in the comments to build a community.

34. BLOGGING WITH AD REVENUE

Blogging is a versatile way to share your thoughts, ability, and stories while earning money through ad revenue, affiliate marketing, and sponsored content.

- **How It Works**: You create written content on a blog platform, covering topics that interest you or attract a specific audience. As your blog gains traffic, you can monetize it through ads (like Google AdSense), affiliate links, and sponsored posts.

- **Earnings Potential**:
  - o Ad revenue can vary widely, with most bloggers earning $10 to $50 for every 1,000 page view through Google AdSense or other ad networks. Successful bloggers can earn thousands per month from sponsored content and affiliate marketing.
  - o **Pro Tip**: Creating high-quality, valuable content can lead to higher traffic and increased revenue. Focus on SEO strategies to drive organic traffic.

- **Platforms to Use**:
  - o **WordPress**: The most popular blogging platform, offering flexibility and many plugins for SEO and monetization.
  - o **Medium**: A great platform for reaching a built-in audience, though monetization options are more limited.
  - o **Google AdSense**: A program that allows you to earn money by displaying ads on your blog.

- **Realistic Expectations**: Depending on your content and marketing efforts, you could earn between $100 and $5,000 monthly within a year of consistent blogging.

- **Getting Started**:
    - **Select a Niche**: Choose a topic you are passionate about and that has an audience. Research potential competitors to find gaps you can fill.
    - **Create Quality Content**: Focus on producing well-researched, engaging, and original content. Consistency is key.
    - **Promote Your Blog**: Use social media, SEO, and email marketing to attract readers. Building an audience takes time and effort.
    - **Monetize Your Blog**: Once you have consistent traffic, apply for ad networks, explore affiliate marketing, and consider sponsored content opportunities.

35. PODCASTING AND GETTING SPONSORS

Podcasting has exploded in popularity, offering a platform for individuals to share their voices, stories, and ability. With minimal startup costs, it can be an accessible way to make money online.

- **How It Works**: You create audio content on a specific topic, which can range from interviews and storytelling to educational content and discussions. As your audience grows, you can monetize through sponsorships, listener donations, and merchandise.

- **Earnings Potential**:
    - Depending on your audience size and engagement, you could earn anywhere from $15 to $50 per 1,000 downloads through sponsorships. Successful podcasters with a significant following can earn thousands per episode.
    - **Pro Tip**: Focus on building a loyal audience and engaging with listeners to increase sponsorship opportunities. Quality content and consistent episodes are crucial for growth.

- **Platforms to Use**:
    - **Anchor**: A free podcast hosting platform that offers monetization options and distribution to major podcast directories like Spotify and Apple Podcasts.
    - **Buzzsprout**: Another popular hosting platform that provides analytics, monetization options, and a user-friendly interface.

- o **Zencastr**: A platform for recording high-quality remote interviews, ideal for podcasters conducting interviews with guests.

- **Realistic Expectations**: With dedication and effective marketing, you could realistically earn between $100 and $5,000 monthly as your podcast grows in popularity.

- **Getting Started**:
  - o **Choose a Topic**: Select a niche that interests you and has an audience. Consider what makes your perspective unique.
  - o **Plan Your Content**: Outline episodes and consider inviting guests to add variety. Consistency in release schedules is essential.
  - o **Record and Edit**: Invest in a good microphone and editing software to ensure quality audio. Edit out mistakes and add intro/outro music to enhance your podcast.
  - o **Promote Your Podcast**: Use social media, podcast directories, and your network to share episodes. Engage with listeners to build a community.

36. SELF-PUBLISHING SHORT BOOKS ON AMAZON KINDLE

The rise of self-publishing has democratized the world of authorship, allowing anyone to share their stories, ability, or knowledge without traditional publishing hurdles. Amazon Kindle Direct Publishing (KDP) is one of the most popular platforms for self-publishing eBooks.

- **How It Works**: You write a short book—be it fiction, non-fiction, guides, or how-tos—and publish it on Amazon Kindle. You can set your pricing, and Amazon pays you a royalty for each sale.

- **Earnings Potential**:
  - o Self-published authors can earn royalties ranging from 35% to 70% per sale, depending on the pricing and distribution options. For a book priced at $2.99, you could earn about $2.09 to $1.05 per sale.
  - o **Pro Tip**: Pricing your book between $2.99 and $9.99 maximizes your royalty percentage. Marketing your book effectively can significantly increase sales.

- **Platforms to Use**:

- o **Amazon Kindle Direct Publishing (KDP)**: This is the main platform for uploading and selling your eBooks. It's user-friendly and offers extensive reach.
- o **Scrivener**: A popular writing tool that helps you organize your writing and export it in various formats for eBook publishing.
- o **Canva**: Use this design tool to create eye-catching book covers that can attract potential readers.

- **Realistic Expectations**: With effective marketing and engaging content, you could earn between $100 and $2,000 monthly. Some authors even scale up too much higher earnings with multiple titles.

- **Getting Started**:
  - o **Choose Your Niche**: Find a subject you are enthusiastic about or that has demand. Research current trends and popular genres on Amazon.
  - o **Write Your Book**: Set aside dedicated time for writing. Ensure your content is well-structured and edited for clarity and quality.
  - o **Design an Eye-Catching Cover**: Your cover is the first impression potential readers have. Make sure it looks professional.
  - o **Publish and Promote**: Once your book is published, promote it through social media, email newsletters, and book review sites. Consider using Amazon's promotional tools for better visibility.

37. REVIEWING PRODUCTS ON A BLOG OR YOUTUBE

Product reviews are incredibly valuable to consumers making purchasing decisions. If you have a knack for providing insightful critiques, you can monetize your opinions through a blog or YouTube channel.

- **How It Works**: You review various products, be they tech gadgets, beauty products, household items, or services—through written posts or video content. Companies often seek reviews to promote their products, and you can earn money through affiliate marketing and sponsorships.

- **Earnings Potential**:
  - o Successful product reviewers can earn from $10 to $100 per review, depending on the product and your audience size. Additionally, affiliate commissions can range from 5% to 50% of the sale price.

- o **Pro Tip**: Focus on building a loyal audience by providing genuine, thorough reviews. Brands are more likely to approach you for collaborations if they see you have a dedicated following.

- **Platforms to Use**:
  - o **WordPress**: Ideal for blogging, it allows you to write detailed reviews and use SEO tools to attract traffic.
  - o **YouTube**: Perfect for video reviews, offering the chance to showcase products in action and engage with your audience through comments.
  - o **Amazon Associates**: This is an affiliate program that allows you to earn commissions by linking products on Amazon within your reviews.

- **Realistic Expectations**: As you build your audience and reputation, you could earn between $100 and $5,000 monthly from product reviews and affiliate sales.

- **Getting Started**:
  - o **Select Your Niche**: Focus on a specific category (tech, beauty, fitness) to build authority. Research products that resonate with your target audience.
  - o **Create Quality Content**: Be honest and thorough in your reviews. Use high-quality images or videos to enhance your posts.
  - o **Promote Your Content**: Share your reviews on social media and engage with your audience to build trust.
  - o **Network with Brands**: Reach out to brands for collaboration opportunities. As your platform grows, they may approach you for partnerships.

38. CREATING AND SELLING PRINTABLES ON ETSY

Selling digital products like printables is a fantastic way to make passive income online. From planners and calendars to artwork and educational materials, the demand for printables continues to grow.

- **How It Works**: You create printable designs using tools like Canva or Adobe Illustrator and sell them on Etsy. Customers download the files and print them at home, allowing you to earn money without worrying about inventory or shipping.

- **Earnings Potential**:

- Pricing for printables can range from $1 to $30, depending on the complexity and value of the product. Successful sellers can earn from $200 to $5,000 monthly based on their product range and marketing efforts.
- **Pro Tip**: Focus on a niche market (like planners for teachers or wedding invitations) to stand out in a crowded marketplace.

- **Platforms to Use**:
    - **Etsy**: The main platform for selling digital printables. It has a large audience looking specifically for unique and creative products.
    - **Canva**: Use this graphic design tool to create visually appealing printables. It's user-friendly and offers many templates to get started.
    - **Creative Market**: Another platform for selling digital products, often frequented by designers and small businesses.
- **Realistic Expectations**: With consistent effort and a well-curated shop, you could realistically earn between $100 and $3,000 monthly, especially if you create a variety of products.
- **Getting Started**:
    - **Choose Your Niche**: Find what type of printables you want to create and who your target audience is.
    - **Create High-Quality Designs**: Focus on originality and utility in your designs. Ensure they are easy to download and print.
    - **Set Up Your Etsy Shop**: Create an engaging shop with a clear description of your products. Use SEO strategies to help your listings appear in search results.
    - **Market Your Printables**: Share your products on social media platforms, consider creating a Pinterest account to showcase your designs, and engage with your audience for feedback.

39. STARTING AN ASMR CHANNEL OR VIDEO SERIES

ASMR (Autonomous Sensory Meridian Response) content has gained immense popularity on platforms like YouTube, where creators provide soothing sounds and visuals to help viewers relax, sleep, or focus. If you have a passion for creating calming experiences, this could be a great avenue for you.

- **How It Works**: You create and share videos featuring ASMR-inducing sounds, such as tapping, whispering, or nature sounds. Viewers typically watch these videos for relaxation or stress relief.
- **Earnings Potential**:
    - Successful ASMR channels can earn through ad revenue, sponsorships, and viewer donations. Earnings vary widely, but channels with a significant following can earn anywhere from $100 to $10,000 monthly.
    - **Pro Tip**: Engage with your audience through comments and community posts to build a loyal following. Consistence in posting is key.
- **Platforms to Use**:
    - **YouTube**: The most popular platform for ASMR content. Monetization options include ads, memberships, and Super Chat.
    - **Twitch**: Some ASMR creators stream live on Twitch, where viewers can subscribe and donate in real time.
    - **Instagram or TikTok**: These platforms can also be used to share short ASMR clips to attract a wider audience.
- **Realistic Expectations**: With a consistent upload schedule and engaging content, you could earn between $100 and $5,000 monthly, depending on your viewer base and engagement rates.
- **Getting Started**:
    - **Invest in Equipment**: A good microphone is crucial for capturing high-quality sounds. Consider investing in a camera for video quality as well.
    - **Choose Your Niche**: Explore different ASMR styles (whispering, roleplay, nature sounds) and find what resonates with you and your potential audience.
    - **Create Quality Content**: Plan your videos carefully, ensuring good sound quality and a calming environment for recording.
    - **Promote Your Channel**: Share your videos on social media, engage with ASMR communities, and collaborate with other creators to grow your audience.

40. HOSTING A PAID NEWSLETTER ON SUBSTACK OR PATREON

In an age of information overload, curated content can be incredibly valuable. By offering a paid newsletter, you can share insights, analysis, and exclusive content with subscribers who are willing to pay for your ability.

- **How It Works**: You create a newsletter focusing on a specific topic or niche, providing valuable information, analysis, or entertainment. Subscribers pay a monthly fee for access to your content.

- **Earnings Potential**:
    - Earnings can vary widely based on your subscriber base. With 100 subscribers paying $5 per month, you'd earn $500 monthly. Successful newsletters can grow to thousands of subscribers, resulting in substantial income.
    - **Pro Tip**: Focus on building an engaged community. The more valuable your content, the more likely subscribers will remain loyal and refer others.

- **Platforms to Use**:
    - **Substack**: This platform is designed for newsletter creators, allowing you to easily manage subscriptions and payments.
    - **Patreon**: You can host exclusive content for your supporters and offer various subscription tiers for different levels of access.
    - **Mailchimp**: For those who prefer more customization, Mailchimp allows you to create and send newsletters to your subscribers.

- **Realistic Expectations**: Depending on your niche and marketing efforts, you could realistically earn between $100 and $5,000 monthly, especially if you can attract a dedicated readership.

- **Getting Started**:
    - **Find Your Niche**: Choose a topic you're passionate about and have expertise in. This could be anything from finance, health, technology, to pop culture.
    - **Create High-Quality Content**: Your newsletters should provide genuine value. Consider including research, expert interviews, and actionable advice.

- o **Promote Your Newsletter**: Use social media, personal networks, and guest appearances on other newsletters or podcasts to grow your subscriber base.
- o **Engage with Your Audience**: Encourage feedback and interaction with your subscribers to create a sense of community around your content.

41. CURATING AND SELLING PHOTO COLLECTIONS

If you have a talent for photography or an eye for visuals, curating and selling photo collections can be a lucrative business. Many businesses and individuals seek high-quality images for their websites, marketing, or personal projects.

- **How It Works**: You curate collections of photos around specific themes or topics and sell them as digital downloads. Customers can use these images for various purposes, from marketing materials to personal projects.

- **Earnings Potential**:
  - o Depending on the quality and uniqueness of your photos, you could sell collections anywhere from $5 to $500. Successful photographers can earn between $200 and $5,000 monthly based on their sales volume.
  - o **Pro Tip**: Focus on niches with high demand, such as lifestyle, food, travel, or nature photography.

- **Platforms to Use**:
  - o **Etsy**: Ideal for selling digital downloads, including curated photo collections. You can set up a shop and market your collections effectively.
  - o **Shutterstock or Adobe Stock**: These platforms allow you to sell your individual images and curated collections to a wide audience.
  - o **Instagram**: Use this platform to showcase your photography and drive traffic to your sales page.

- **Realistic Expectations**: If you market your collections effectively and produce high-quality images, you could earn between $100 and $2,000 monthly.

- **Getting Started**:
  - o **Build Your Portfolio**: Start by taking high-quality photos that reflect your style and niche. Curate collections that are visually appealing and thematically cohesive.

- **Choose Your Sales Platforms**: Decide where you want to sell your photos and set up your accounts.
- **Market Your Collections**: Use social media to showcase your work, collaborate with other photographers, and engage with communities interested in your niche.
- **Offer Unique Products**: Consider creating themed photo packs or bundles that appeal to specific customer needs, such as seasonal promotions or business-focused collections.

42. CREATING SIMPLE, LOW-CONTENT BOOKS (E.G., JOURNALS, PLANNERS) ON AMAZON KDP

Amazon Kindle Direct Publishing (KDP) offers an accessible platform for aspiring authors and creators to publish low-content books such as journals, planners, and notebooks. These books require minimal writing but can be incredibly popular.

- **How It Works**: Low-content books can include lined journals, daily planners, gratitude journals, coloring books, and more. You design the interior and cover, then upload it to KDP, where it can be sold as both a physical book and a digital download.

- **Earnings Potential**:
  - Depending on your niche and marketing efforts, you could earn anywhere from $1 to $5 per book sold. Successful sellers with multiple titles can earn between $200 and $5,000 monthly.
  - **Pro Tip**: Focus on specific niches (e.g., mindfulness journals, workout planners) to appeal to target audiences.

- **Platforms to Use**:
  - **Amazon KDP**: The primary platform for self-publishing your low-content books, allowing you to reach millions of potential customers.
  - **Canva**: A user-friendly design tool that can help you create visually appealing interiors and covers for your books.
  - **Creative Fabrica**: A resource for buying design elements and templates for your books.

- **Realistic Expectations**: With consistent effort in marketing and quality design, you could realistically earn between $100 and $2,000 monthly.

- **Getting Started**:
  - **Research Your Niche**: Explore popular trends on Amazon to find niches that have demand but are not overly saturated.
  - **Design Your Book**: Use Canva or other design tools to create your interiors and covers. Ensure your designs are appealing and functional.
  - **Publish on KDP**: Follow Amazon's guidelines to upload your book, set your pricing, and select your distribution options.
  - **Market Your Books**: Promote your titles on social media, use SEO strategies to perfect your listings, and consider running ads on Amazon to boost visibility.

CHAPTER 5:
MONEY FROM MARKETPLACES – EASY WAYS TO SELL DIGITAL GOODS

43. SELLING STOCK VIDEOS

The demand for video content is skyrocketing, with businesses, marketers, and content creators constantly looking for high-quality stock videos. If you have a knack for videography, this could be a profitable venture.

- **How It Works**: You create and upload high-quality video footage to stock video platforms. Customers can buy licenses to use your videos for various projects, from advertising to social media content.

- **Earnings Potential**:
    - Depending on the platform and your video quality, you could earn anywhere from $1 to $200 per video download. Top contributors can earn between $500 and $5,000 monthly.
    - **Pro Tip**: Focus on trending topics or industries (e.g., lifestyle, nature, business) to maximize sales potential.

- **Platforms to Use**:
    - **Shutterstock**: A leading platform for stock videos, where you can earn a commission each time your video is downloaded.
    - **Adobe Stock**: Another popular platform that allows you to sell both videos and photos, with a competitive payout structure.
    - **Pond5**: Specializes in stock media, including videos, and offers a generous payout percentage.

- **Realistic Expectations**: If you consistently upload high-quality footage and promote your work, you could realistically earn between $100 and $2,000 monthly.

- **Getting Started**:
    - **Invest in Quality Equipment**: A good camera and stabilizer can significantly improve the quality of your footage.
    - **Create Diverse Content**: Shoot a variety of scenes that could appeal to different markets, including b-roll, lifestyle shots, and scenic views.

- o **Perfect for SEO**: Use relevant keywords and tags when uploading your videos to help potential buyers find your work.
- o **Promote Your Videos**: Share your work on social media and consider building a portfolio website to showcase your best footage.

44. OFFERING PERSONALIZED VIDEO MESSAGES ON CAMEO

Cameo is a platform where fans can pay for personalized video messages from celebrities and influencers. If you have a unique personality, ability, or following, you could also monetize this trend.

- **How It Works**: You create personalized video messages for fans on Cameo. These messages can be for birthdays, anniversaries, or special occasions, and buyers can select their favorite creators to send the message.

- **Earnings Potential**:
  - o Prices for personalized videos can range from $10 to over $1,000, depending on your popularity and demand. Many creators earn between $100 and $5,000 monthly, depending on how many messages they sell.
  - o **Pro Tip**: Personalization is key—make each message special and tailored to the buyer's request to encourage repeat purchases.

- **Platforms to Use**:
  - o **Cameo**: The primary platform for selling personalized video messages. Create an account and set your pricing based on your popularity and demand.
  - o **Social Media**: Promote your Cameo account on platforms like Instagram, TikTok, or YouTube to reach a larger audience.
  - o **YouTube**: If you have a YouTube channel, you can drive traffic to your Cameo profile by creating videos about the messages you offer.

- **Realistic Expectations**: With a strong following and engaging personality, you could earn between $200 and $5,000 monthly.

- **Getting Started**:

- **Set Up Your Cameo Account**: Create your profile, add a bio, and upload a sample video to showcase your style and personality.
- **Market Yourself**: Use social media to promote your Cameo profile, share examples of your messages, and engage with potential customers.
- **Delivery Quality**: Make each personalized message heartfelt and unique to create a memorable experience for the buyer.
- **Collect Reviews**: Encourage customers to leave positive feedback, as this can help attract more buyers to your profile.

45. SELLING INSTAGRAM STORIES OR POST TEMPLATES

With the rise of social media marketing, many brands and individuals are seeking eye-catching templates to enhance their Instagram presence. If you have a flair for design, creating and selling Instagram templates can be a lucrative venture.

- **How It Works**: You create visually appealing Instagram stories or post templates that users can customize with their own content. These templates are typically sold as digital downloads, allowing customers to easily edit them in design software.

- **Earnings Potential**:
  - Depending on the complexity and uniqueness of your templates, you can charge anywhere from $5 to $50 per template pack. Successful designers can earn between $500 and $5,000 monthly.
  - **Pro Tip**: Focus on trendy themes, such as seasonal designs, minimalist aesthetics, or specific niches (e.g., fitness, fashion) to attract more customers.

- **Platforms to Use**:
  - **Etsy**: A popular marketplace for selling digital downloads, including Instagram templates. Create a shop and promote your listings.
  - **Creative Market**: A platform specifically for designers to sell digital products, including templates for various applications.
  - **Gumroad**: Allows you to sell digital products directly to your audience, with easy-to-use features for managing sales and customer interactions.

- **Realistic Expectations**: With consistent quality and marketing efforts, you could realistically earn between $100 and $2,000 monthly.

- **Getting Started**:
  - **Design Your Templates**: Use design tools like Canva, Adobe Illustrator, or Photoshop to create aesthetically pleasing templates that are easy to customize.
  - **Market Your Products**: Use social media to showcase your templates, share previews, and engage with potential customers.
  - **Improve Your Listings**: Use relevant keywords in your product titles and descriptions to improve visibility on platforms like Etsy and Creative Market.
  - **Bundle Products**: Consider offering bundles of templates at a discount to encourage larger purchases.

46. CREATING AND SELLING SIMPLE WEBSITE THEMES ON WORDPRESS

As businesses and individuals continue to set up their online presence, the demand for user-friendly and visually appealing WordPress themes is ever-growing. If you have web design skills, this could be a profitable opportunity.

- **How It Works**: You create WordPress themes that users can install on their websites. These themes can be sold as standalone products or offered with ongoing support and updates.

- **Earnings Potential**:
  - Prices for WordPress themes can range from $20 to $100 or more, depending on the complexity and features. Established theme developers can earn between $1,000 and $10,000 monthly.
  - **Pro Tip**: Research current trends in web design and user experience to create themes that meet market demands.

- **Platforms to Use**:
  - **ThemeForest**: A leading marketplace for selling WordPress themes, offering a wide audience of potential buyers.
  - **Creative Market**: Another platform where you can sell digital products, including WordPress themes.

- o **Your Own Website**: Create a dedicated website to showcase and sell your themes directly to customers, allowing for greater control over pricing and branding.

- **Realistic Expectations**: With a few quality themes and effective marketing, you could realistically earn between $500 and $5,000 monthly.

- **Getting Started**:
  - o **Learn Theme Development**: Familiarize yourself with WordPress theme development through online courses or tutorials. Understand HTML, CSS, PHP, and JavaScript.
  - o **Create a Unique Theme**: Develop a theme that stands out from the competition, focusing on functionality, design, and user experience.
  - o **Assess and Optimize**: Ensure your theme is compatible with various plugins and responsive across devices. Gather feedback from beta testers to make improvements.
  - o **Market Your Themes**: Use social media, SEO, and online communities to promote your themes and drive traffic to your listings.

47. SELLING ICONS, EMOJIS, OR ILLUSTRATIONS ON CREATIVE MARKET

The demand for unique digital assets like icons, emojis, and illustrations is growing, with designers and businesses seeking creative visuals for their projects. If you have artistic skills, selling these assets can be a lucrative business.

- **How It Works**: You create and sell digital assets, such as sets of icons, custom emojis, or unique illustrations, that users can buy for their websites, apps, and marketing materials.

- **Earnings Potential**:
  - o Depending on the complexity and quality, you can charge anywhere from $5 to $100 for sets of icons or illustrations. Successful sellers can earn between $300 and $3,000 monthly.
  - o **Pro Tip**: Create themed collections (e.g., seasonal icons, holiday illustrations) to attract buyers looking for specific styles.

- **Platforms to Use**:

- o **Creative Market**: A leading marketplace for designers to sell digital assets, including icons and illustrations.
- o **Etsy**: Another popular platform where you can sell digital downloads, including your creative assets.
- o **Envato Elements**: A subscription-based service where users pay for access to a library of assets, allowing you to earn money from your designs.
- **Realistic Expectations**: With consistent quality and marketing, you could realistically earn between $200 and $2,000 monthly.
- **Getting Started**:
  - o **Develop Your Style**: Focus on creating a unique artistic style that sets your work apart from others.
  - o **Create Quality Assets**: Use software like Adobe Illustrator or Procreate to create high-quality icons and illustrations.
  - o **Perfect Your Listings**: Use relevant keywords in your product descriptions and titles to improve visibility in search results.
  - o **Promote Your Work**: Use social media, design forums, and online communities to showcase your designs and attract buyers.

48. SELLING YOUR DIGITAL ARTWORK AS NFTS

The NFT (Non-Fungible Token) market has exploded in recent years, offering artists a unique opportunity to sell their digital artwork directly to buyers. NFTs are blockchain-based tokens that verify the ownership and authenticity of digital items, allowing you to sell your art as a unique digital asset.

- **How It Works**: You create digital artwork and mint it as an NFT on a blockchain platform. Once minted, you can list it for sale in various NFT marketplaces.
- **Earnings Potential**:
  - o The price of NFTs varies widely based on the artist's reputation and the uniqueness of the work. Some artists have sold NFTs for millions, while others may sell theirs for a few dollars.
  - o **Pro Tip**: Building a strong online presence and marketing your art effectively can significantly increase your sales potential.

- **Platforms to Use**:
    - **OpenSea**: One of the largest NFT marketplaces, allowing you to mint and sell your digital art easily.
    - **Rarible**: A decentralized platform where artists can create and sell NFTs, with a user-friendly interface.
    - **Mintable**: A platform that allows you to create NFTs without needing extensive blockchain knowledge.
- **Realistic Expectations**: While some artists achieve significant success, it's crucial to understand that NFT sales can be unpredictable. With proper marketing and unique artwork, you could earn anywhere from $100 to $10,000 per piece.
- **Getting Started**:
    - **Create Your Artwork**: Use digital art software like Adobe Photoshop or Procreate to design your unique pieces.
    - **Choose a Blockchain**: Decide on the blockchain you want to mint your NFT on, with Ethereum being the most popular.
    - **Mint Your NFT**: Follow the platform's instructions to upload your artwork, set your price, and mint your NFT.
    - **Promote Your Art**: Share your NFTs on social media and engage with potential buyers to create buzz around your work.

49. CREATING CUSTOM STICKERS FOR MESSAGING APPS

As messaging apps grow in popularity, custom stickers have become a fun way for users to express themselves. Creating and selling custom stickers can be a rewarding and profitable venture if you have a creative flair.

- **How It Works**: You design a set of custom stickers that users can buy and use in their messaging apps. These stickers can be sold individually or as packs.
- **Earnings Potential**:
    - Sticker packs typically sell for $1 to $5, depending on the number of stickers in the pack. Successful sticker creators can earn between $100 and $2,000 monthly.

- o **Pro Tip**: Focus on trends and themes that resonate with users, such as seasonal stickers, pop culture references, or niche interests.
- **Platforms to Use**:
  - o **Etsy**: A popular marketplace for digital downloads, including custom sticker packs.
  - o **Telegram**: You can create and share sticker packs directly on this messaging platform, allowing users to download and use your creations.
  - o **LINE Creators Market**: A platform dedicated to selling stickers for the LINE messaging app, which is very popular in certain regions.
- **Realistic Expectations**: With quality designs and effective marketing, you could realistically earn between $50 and $1,000 monthly.
- **Getting Started**:
  - o **Design Your Stickers**: Use graphic design software like Adobe Illustrator or Canva to create appealing and fun stickers.
  - o **Choose Your Platform**: Decide where you want to sell your stickers, based on your target audience.
  - o **Market Your Stickers**: Promote your sticker packs on social media and through influencer collaborations to reach a larger audience.
  - o **Engage with Customers**: Respond to feedback and create new designs based on customer requests to build loyalty.

50. SELLING ONLINE COURSES ON SIMPLE TOPICS

Online learning has surged in popularity and selling courses on platforms like Udemy or Teachable allows you to share your knowledge with others while earning passive income. You don't need to be an expert; even simple topics can attract learners.

- **How It Works**: You create a course covering a specific topic, which can be anything from gardening to basic coding, and host it on an online learning platform.
- **Earnings Potential**:
  - o Course prices typically range from $10 to $200, and depending on the course's success, you can earn anywhere from $100 to $10,000 monthly.

- - **Pro Tip**: Choose a topic you are knowledgeable about and enthusiastic about, as this will resonate with learners and enhance the quality of your course.

- **Platforms to Use**:

  - **Udemy**: A popular platform for selling online courses, offering extensive marketing and student engagement tools.
  - **Teachable**: Allows you to create and sell courses directly, giving you more control over branding and pricing.
  - **Skillshare**: Focused on creative courses, where you earn money based on the number of minutes watched.

- **Realistic Expectations**: With a well-designed course and effective marketing, you could realistically earn between $500 and $5,000 monthly.

- **Getting Started**:

  - **Choose a Course Topic**: Find a subject you're knowledgeable about that has a potential audience.
  - **Create Course Content**: Develop engaging video lectures, quizzes, and supplemental materials to enhance the learning experience.
  - **Market Your Course**: Use social media, email marketing, and online communities to promote your course to potential students.
  - **Gather Feedback**: Encourage students to leave reviews and provide feedback to improve your course and attract new learners.

51. PUBLISHING MUSIC AND SOUND EFFECTS ON AUDIOJUNGLE

AudioJungle is a marketplace where musicians and sound designers can sell their music tracks and sound effects. This is a fantastic opportunity for anyone with a knack for music composition or sound design to generate passive income.

- **How It Works**: You create original music tracks or sound effects, upload them to AudioJungle, and set a price for each item. When customers buy your music or sound effects, you earn a royalty based on the sale price.

- **Earnings Potential**:

  - Prices for music tracks typically range from $10 to $50, while sound effects can sell for $1 to $20 each.

- Established contributors can earn hundreds to thousands of dollars monthly, depending on the quality and popularity of their offerings.
- **Pro Tip**: High-quality audio files with clear sound and engaging content tend to attract more buyers.

- **Platforms to Use**:
    - **AudioJungle**: The main platform for selling your music and sound effects. It's part of the Envato Market, known for a wide range of creative assets.
    - **Pond5**: Another marketplace for selling stock audio, offering a broader audience for your sound creations.
    - **PremiumBeat**: A curated library that focuses on high-quality music for filmmakers, which could be another avenue for selling your work.
- **Realistic Expectations**: New contributors might earn around $50 to $200 in their first month, while experienced salespeople could see earnings of $500 to $2,000 or more, depending on their portfolio size and marketing efforts.
- **Getting Started**:
    - **Create Your Music or Sound Effects**: Use digital audio workstations (DAWs) like Logic Pro, Ableton Live, or FL Studio to compose and record your audio.
    - **Prepare Your Files**: Ensure your tracks are high quality, properly mixed, and edited for clarity.
    - **Set Up Your AudioJungle Account**: Create an account on AudioJungle and familiarize yourself with the submission guidelines and requirements.
    - **Upload and Promote Your Tracks**: Once uploaded, promote your music on social media, YouTube, and other platforms to drive traffic to your AudioJungle portfolio.

52. SELLING PRESET FILTERS FOR PHOTOS (INSTAGRAM, LIGHTROOM)

With the rise of social media platforms like Instagram, many users seek ways to enhance their photos quickly and easily. Selling preset filters can be a lucrative business, especially if you have a good eye for aesthetics and design.

- **How It Works**: You create preset filters that users can apply to their photos in editing apps like Adobe Lightroom or Instagram. These presets can transform the look of an image with just one click.

- **Earnings Potential**:
    - Presets typically sell for $5 to $50 per pack, and with the right marketing, you can earn $200 to $2,000 monthly.
    - **Pro Tip**: Offer a range of styles (vintage, bright, moody) to appeal to different audiences and trends.
- **Platforms to Use**:
    - **Etsy**: A popular marketplace for selling digital products, including photo presets.
    - **Gumroad**: A straightforward platform for selling digital downloads directly to your audience.
    - **Creative Market**: An online marketplace where you can sell design resources, including Lightroom presets.
- **Realistic Expectations**: New sellers might earn $50 to $300 monthly, while successful creators with an established audience could see earnings in the $1,000 to $5,000 range.
- **Getting Started**:
    - **Create Your Presets**: Use Adobe Lightroom to design filters that enhance photos. Save the presets for easy sharing.
    - **Choose Your Selling Platform**: Decide where you want to sell your presets based on your target audience.
    - **Market Your Presets**: Use social media platforms, particularly Instagram, to showcase before-and-after photos using your presets. Collaborate with influencers for greater reach.
    - **Engage with Your Audience**: Create tutorial videos proving how to use your presets and engage with customers to build a loyal following.

CHAPTER 6:
ONLINE GAMING AND REWARDS – FUN AND PROFITABLE ACTIVITIES

53. EARNING THROUGH IN-GAME TRADING (E.G., SKINS, ITEMS)

In-game trading has become a popular way for gamers to monetize their gaming experience. Many games, especially first-person shooters and battle royale games, offer virtual items such as skins, weapons, and character outfits that can be bought, sold, or traded.

- **How It Works**: Players earn or purchase in-game items and then trade or sell them on various platforms or marketplaces. The value of items can fluctuate based on demand, rarity, and market trends.

- **Earnings Potential**:
    - Some rare skins or items can sell for significant amounts, sometimes hundreds or thousands of dollars.
    - **Pro Tip**: Staying informed about game updates, item rarity, and market trends can help you find valuable items to trade.

- **Platforms to Use**:
    - **Steam Community Market**: A marketplace for buying and selling in-game items for games like CS and Dota 2.
    - **OPSkins**: A third-party marketplace for trading and selling skins from various games.
    - **CS. MONEY**: A platform for trading CS skins where players can exchange their items for others or cash out.

- **Realistic Expectations**: While some players make a few dollars here and there, resolute traders can earn anywhere from $50 to $500 monthly, depending on their trading strategies and the games they focus on.

- **Getting Started**:
    - **Choose Your Game**: Focus on games that have a vibrant marketplace for trading items, such as CS, Dota 2, or Fortnite.

- o **Start Earning Items**: Play the game regularly, complete challenges, or buy items to build a collection.
- o **Trade Strategically**: Check market prices and trade items wisely to maximize your earnings.
- o **Leverage Marketplaces**: Use platforms like Steam Community Market to sell items directly to other players.

54. PARTICIPATING IN ONLINE GAMING TOURNAMENTS

With the rise of eSports, online gaming tournaments have become a lucrative way for skilled players to earn money. Many games host tournaments with cash prizes, sponsorships, and streaming opportunities.

- **How It Works**: Players can enter tournaments that often require an entry fee, with the potential to win cash prizes based on performance. Some tournaments are casual, while others are highly competitive.

- **Earnings Potential**:
  - o Prizes vary by tournament, ranging from $50 for smaller competitions to thousands of dollars for larger, sponsored events.
  - o **Pro Tip**: Joining teams or communities can help you find tournaments and improve your skills through practice and collaboration.

- **Platforms to Use**:
  - o **Battlefy**: A platform for organizing and finding tournaments across various games.
  - o **Toornament**: Another platform that hosts gaming tournaments and allows players to sign up for competitions.
  - o **Challengermode**: A platform for competitive gaming that connects players with tournaments in various games.

- **Realistic Expectations**: Beginners might earn $50 to $200 from smaller tournaments, while seasoned players can earn several thousand dollars per month by consistently performing well.

- **Getting Started**:

- o **Choose Your Game**: Focus on games with active eSports scenes, such as League of Legends, Fortnite, or Dota 2.
- o **Practice and Improve**: Regularly play to hone your skills and learn strategies.
- o **Join Tournaments**: Sign up for online tournaments that match your skill level and keep an eye on competitive events in the gaming community.
- o **Network**: Connect with other players to form teams and enter team-based tournaments.

55. SELLING YOUR GAMING ACCOUNTS OR ITEMS

As gamers invest time and money into their accounts, selling them can be a practical way to recoup some of that investment. This can include accounts with rare items, high levels, or unique skins.

- **How It Works**: Players can sell their gaming accounts, character skins, or valuable in-game items directly to other players or through specialized marketplaces.
- **Earnings Potential**:
  - o The price of accounts can range widely based on the game's popularity and the account's features, from $20 for basic accounts to several hundred dollars for accounts with rare items or high-level characters.
  - o **Pro Tip**: Ensure that you follow the game's terms of service to avoid any issues when selling your account.
- **Platforms to Use**:
  - o **PlayerUp**: A marketplace for buying and selling gaming accounts and in-game items across various games.
  - o **G2G**: A platform for gamers to trade accounts and items, with secure payment options.
  - o **EpicNPC**: A forum dedicated to buying and selling gaming accounts and items, where you can find interested buyers.
- **Realistic Expectations**: Depending on the game's market and the account's value, you might earn anywhere from $50 to $500 per account.
- **Getting Started**:

- **Evaluate Your Account**: Assess the value of your gaming account based on level, achievements, and rare items.
- **Choose a Selling Platform**: Decide where you want to sell your account, ensuring it's a reputable marketplace.
- **List Your Account**: Create a detailed listing highlighting the account's features and any unique items.
- **Negotiate and Complete the Sale**: Communicate with potential buyers, negotiate a price, and complete the sale safely.

56. BETA-TESTING NEW VIDEO GAMES

Beta-testing involves playing a game before its official release to find bugs, glitches, and other issues. Developers often pay beta testers or offer them in-game rewards for their feedback.

- **How It Works**: Players are invited to evaluate a game during its beta phase. They provide feedback on gameplay, mechanics, and any issues they meet. This helps developers improve the game before launch.

- **Earnings Potential**:
    - Many developers offer compensation in the form of cash, gift cards, or in-game currency. While some beta tests are unpaid, paid opportunities can range from $10 to $50 per hour, depending on the game's scope and the tester's experience.
    - **Pro Tip**: Joining beta testing communities can increase your chances of being selected for more lucrative testing opportunities.

- **Platforms to Use**:
    - **PlaytestCloud**: Connects game developers with beta testers, offering compensation for feedback.
    - **BetaTesting**: A platform where testers can sign up for beta-testing opportunities and provide feedback on various applications, including games.
    - **Gaming Communities and Forums**: Sites like Reddit or specialized gaming forums often have posts by developers seeking beta testers.

- **Realistic Expectations**: Beginners might earn around $50 to $200 per game evaluated, while experienced testers working on larger projects could make $500 or more per project.

- **Getting Started**:
  - **Sign Up for Platforms**: Register on beta testing platforms and create a profile highlighting your gaming experience.
  - **Join Gaming Communities**: Take part in forums and social media groups to find beta testing opportunities.
  - **Evaluate Games and Provide Feedback**: Once selected, play the game thoroughly and provide detailed feedback to help developers improve the final product.

57. STREAMING GAMEPLAY ON TWITCH

Twitch is a live-streaming platform primarily focused on gaming. Streamers broadcast their gameplay to audiences in real time and can earn money through subscriptions, donations, and sponsorships.

- **How It Works**: Streamers set up a channel, choose games to play, and engage with their audience during live broadcasts. As they grow their following, they can monetize their streams through various means.

- **Earnings Potential**:
  - Streamers can earn money through subscriptions (monthly fees paid by viewers), donations, and ad revenue. Successful streamers can be made anywhere from a few hundred dollars to thousands per month.
  - **Pro Tip**: Consistency in streaming schedule and engaging with your audience are key to building a loyal viewer base.

- **Platforms to Use**:
  - **Twitch**: The primary platform for game streaming, offering various monetization options through affiliate and partner programs.
  - **YouTube Gaming**: Another platform where gamers can stream and monetize their gameplay through ads and memberships.
  - **Facebook Gaming**: A growing platform for game streaming, giving monetization options to creators.

- **Realistic Expectations**: New streamers might earn $50 to $200 monthly as they build their audience, while set up streamers can earn from $1,000 to $10,000 or more per month.

- **Getting Started**:

- o **Create a Twitch Account**: Set up your channel and customize it to reflect your gaming style.
- o **Invest in Equipment**: Get a good-quality microphone, webcam, and gaming setup for a professional streaming experience.
- o **Choose Your Games**: Select games that you enjoy and that have a strong viewer interest.
- o **Engage with Your Audience**: Interact with viewers through chat and social media to build a community around your channel.

58. CREATING GUIDES OR WALKTHROUGHS FOR POPULAR GAMES

Game guides and walkthroughs help players navigate challenging levels or learn strategies to improve their gameplay. This can be a great way to earn money if you have a knack for explaining game mechanics and strategies.

- **How It Works**: You create detailed guides, tutorials, or walkthroughs and share them through blogs, YouTube, or eBooks. Monetization can come from ads, sponsorships, or selling the guides directly.

- **Earnings Potential**:
  - o Successful guides can generate revenue through ad placements, affiliate marketing, and selling guides. Earnings can range from $100 to $1,000 monthly, depending on traffic and engagement.
  - o **Pro Tip**: Focus on popular games and trending topics to attract more viewers and readers.

- **Platforms to Use**:
  - o **YouTube**: Create video walkthroughs and monetize them through ads and sponsorships.
  - o **Medium**: Publish written guides and earn through the Medium Partner Program.
  - o **Amazon Kindle**: Self-publish eBooks with guides and tutorials for popular games.

- **Realistic Expectations**: Beginners might earn $50 to $300 per month from guides, while experienced creators can see earnings of $1,000 or more, especially if they build a large following.

- **Getting Started**:

- o **Choose Your Game**: Focus on games that are currently popular or have a strong community.
- o **Research Common Challenges**: Find areas where players struggle and create content that addresses those challenges.
- o **Create Your Guides**: Use a mix of written, video, and visual content to make your guides engaging.
- o **Promote Your Content**: Share your guides on social media, gaming forums, and communities to attract viewers and readers.

59. PLAYING ONLINE FANTASY SPORTS

Fantasy sports allow players to create virtual teams composed of real-life athletes and compete based on their performance in actual games. This exciting avenue not only evaluates your sports knowledge but can also be profitable.

- **How It Works**: Players draft athletes to form their teams. The performance of these athletes in real games translates into points, deciding the team's success in various leagues or contests.

- **Earnings Potential**:
  - o Depending on the league and the buy-in amounts, earnings can vary widely. Casual players might earn small amounts, while serious players can win substantial cash prizes, sometimes in the thousands of dollars.
  - o **Pro Tip**: Understanding player statistics, injuries, and game matchups is crucial for success in fantasy sports.

- **Platforms to Use**:
  - o **DraftKings**: A leading platform for daily fantasy sports, offering contests across various sports, including football, basketball, and baseball.
  - o **FanDuel**: Another popular daily fantasy sports site, known for its user-friendly interface and a wide range of contests.
  - o **Yahoo Fantasy Sports**: Provides a robust platform for both daily and season-long fantasy sports, with various league formats.

- **Realistic Expectations**: New players can expect to start small, perhaps earning $20 to $100 initially as they learn the ropes. More experienced players, especially those in larger contests, can win from $1,000 to $10,000 or more depending on their skill level and the stakes.

- **Getting Started**:
    - **Choose Your Sport**: Select a sport you're passionate about, as this will enhance your experience and performance.
    - **Research Players**: Analyze player statistics, trends, and injuries to make informed decisions during your drafts.
    - **Join Leagues**: Start with smaller leagues to get a feel for the game before entering high-stakes contests.
    - **Engage with Communities**: Join forums or social media groups where fantasy sports enthusiasts discuss strategies and share tips.

60. COMPLETING GAMING CHALLENGES ON REWARD PLATFORMS

Several online platforms reward users for completing gaming challenges, evaluating your skills, and earning cash or gift cards in return.

- **How It Works**: Users sign up on reward platforms and complete various gaming challenges or tasks. These tasks can range from playing specific games to achieving particular in-game milestones. Upon successful completion, users earn rewards.

- **Earnings Potential**: While individual challenges may pay small amounts, regular participation can add up over time. Players can typically earn between $1 to $10 per challenge, with some platforms offering bonus rewards for consistent engagement.
    - **Pro Tip**: Focus on platforms that offer challenges for games you already play or enjoy to maximize your earnings.

- **Platforms to Use**:
    - **Mistplay**: A loyalty program for gamers where users earn points by playing and testing new games. Points can be redeemed for gift cards to popular retailers.
    - **Lucktastic**: An app that allows users to play scratch-off lottery games, with chances to win cash prizes and tokens that can be redeemed for rewards.

- **Swagbucks**: While primarily known for surveys, Swagbucks also offers rewards for playing games and completing challenges.
- **Realistic Expectations**: Beginners might earn around $5 to $30 a month from occasional challenges, while more engaged users could see earnings rise to $100 or more monthly as they complete multiple tasks.
- **Getting Started**:
    - **Sign Up for Platforms**: Register on popular reward platforms and set up your profile.
    - **Explore Challenges**: Browse through available challenges and select those that interest you.
    - **Stay Consistent**: Regularly take part in challenges to maximize your rewards and earnings.
    - **Redeem Your Rewards**: Once you've accumulated enough points or earnings, redeem them for cash or gift cards.

CHAPTER 7:
PEER-TO-PEER PLATFORMS – GET PAID TO SHARE WHAT YOU ALREADY HAVE

61. RENTING YOUR CAR WITH TURO

Turo is a peer-to-peer car rental platform that allows you to rent out your vehicle to others. If you have a car that you don't use every day, this could be an excellent way to earn some extra cash.

- **How It Works**: Car owners list their vehicles on Turo, setting their rental prices and availability. Renters browse available cars, select one, and make a booking. Turo provides insurance coverage during the rental period.

- **Earnings Potential**:
    - Rental prices depend on the car's make, model, location, and demand. On average, car owners can earn between $30 to $100 per day. Luxury and specialty cars can command even higher rates.
    - **Pro Tip**: Providing excellent customer service and keeping a clean, well-maintained vehicle can lead to positive reviews and repeat renters.

- **Platforms to Use**:
    - **Turo**: The primary platform for renting out your car, with a straightforward listing process and built-in insurance coverage.
    - **Getaround**: Another peer-to-peer car-sharing service where users can rent their vehicles, often with more flexible hourly rates.

- **Realistic Expectations**: Depending on the demand in your area, renting out your car can generate a monthly income ranging from $300 to $1,500. This varies significantly based on how often the car is rented.

- **Getting Started**:
    - **Sign Up on Turo**: Create an account and list your car with detailed descriptions and high-quality photos.
    - **Set Competitive Rates**: Research similar listings in your area to determine a competitive rental price.
    - **Keep Your Car Clean and Well-Maintained**: A well-maintained car attracts more renters and earns better reviews.

- o **Respond Promptly**: Quick responses to inquiries can increase your chances of securing rentals.

62. OFFERING STORAGE SPACE ON NEIGHBOR.COM

Neighbor.com is a platform that connects people with extra storage space to those in need of storage. If you have an unused garage, basement, or spare room, you can rent it out for extra income.

- **How It Works**: Hosts list their available storage space on Neighbor.com, setting their rental prices and availability. Renters can browse listings, contact hosts, and arrange to store their belongings.

- **Earnings Potential**:
  - o The potential earnings vary widely depending on location and space type. On average, hosts can earn between $50 to $300 per month for renting out storage space. Larger spaces or locations in urban areas can command higher rates.
  - o **Pro Tip**: Ensure your storage area is clean, secure, and accessible to make it more attractive to potential renters.

- **Platforms to Use**:
  - o **Neighbor.com**: The primary platform for renting storage space, offering insurance options and a user-friendly interface.
  - o **StoreAtMyHouse**: Similar to Neighbor.com, allowing users to list their storage space for rent.

- **Realistic Expectations**: Depending on the size and type of space you have available, you could earn anywhere from $100 to $500 per month by renting out storage.

- **Getting Started**:
  - o **Sign Up on Neighbor.com**: Create an account and list your available storage space, including photos and descriptions.
  - o **Set Competitive Rates**: Check similar listings to determine a fair price for your space.
  - o **Maintain Security**: Ensure the storage area is secure to build trust with potential renters.
  - o **Be Clear on Terms**: Specify what items are allowed in your space and any access restrictions.

63. RENTING OUT ITEMS LIKE CAMERAS OR DRONES

If you own equipment like cameras, drones, or tools that you don't use frequently, consider renting them out. This can be a lucrative way to monetize your assets.

- **How It Works**: You list your items for rent on various peer-to-peer rental platforms. Renters browse the listings, choose the equipment they need, and make a booking for a specified period.

- **Earnings Potential**:
    - Rental prices can vary based on the item's type, condition, and demand. For example, renting out a camera can yield $20 to $50 per day, while drones can rent for $30 to $100 per day.
    - **Pro Tip**: Provide clear, high-quality images of your items, along with detailed descriptions and usage instructions, to attract more renters.

- **Platforms to Use**:
    - **ShareGrid**: A platform dedicated to renting out camera and video equipment, connecting filmmakers and photographers with gear owners.
    - **Fat Llama**: A peer-to-peer rental marketplace where users can rent out various items, including cameras, drones, and more.
    - **SnapGoods**: Another platform for renting out personal items, allowing users to list and rent cameras and other equipment.

- **Realistic Expectations**: Depending on your item's value and demand, you could earn $100 to $500 monthly by renting out equipment you rarely use.

- **Getting Started**:
    - **Choose Your Platform**: Select a rental platform that caters to your equipment type.
    - **Create a Listing**: Write a detailed description of your item, including its features, condition, and rental price.
    - **Set Clear Terms**: Outline rental duration, deposit requirements, and any insurance options available.

- **Maintain Your Equipment**: Keep your items in excellent condition to ensure positive reviews and repeat rentals.

64. PEER-TO-PEER LENDING

Peer-to-peer (P2P) lending platforms connect borrowers with individual investors who are willing to lend money, allowing you to earn interest on your investments.

- **How It Works**: Investors lend money directly to borrowers through an online platform, bypassing traditional banks. Borrowers may seek loans for various reasons, such as consolidating debt or financing a project. You earn interest on the loan as the borrower makes repayments.

- **Earnings Potential**:
    - P2P lending can offer attractive returns, typically ranging from 5% to 12% annually, depending on the risk level of the borrower. Higher-risk loans can yield higher returns, but they also carry a greater chance of default.
    - **Pro Tip**: Diversifying your investments across multiple loans can help mitigate risks.

- **Platforms to Use**:
    - **Lending Club**: One of the largest P2P lending platforms, offering personal loans, business loans, and auto refinancing.
    - **Prosper**: Another popular platform, focusing on personal loans, where investors can fund loans starting at $25.
    - **Upstart**: Uses advanced algorithms to assess borrower risk, offering a variety of loan types.

- **Realistic Expectations**: While some investors may earn substantial returns, it's important to note that not all loans are repaid. Beginners can start with small amounts, potentially earning a few hundred dollars per year in interest, while experienced investors can see returns in the thousands.

- **Getting Started**:
    - **Sign Up on a P2P Lending Platform**: Create an account and link your bank account.
    - **Fund Your Account**: Deposit funds to start lending.

- o **Choose Loans to Invest In**: Review borrower profiles and select loans based on risk assessment and expected returns.
- o **Monitor Your Investments**: Regularly check on your loans' performance and reinvest repayments to compound your earnings.

65. RENTING OUT BABY GEAR TO TRAVELERS

Renting out baby gear to families traveling with infants or toddlers can be a profitable venture. Many parents prefer renting gear instead of bringing bulky items on trips.

- **How It Works**: You list baby gear—such as cribs, strollers, car seats, and high chairs—on rental platforms. Travelers can browse your listings and rent the items for the duration of their stay.

- **Earnings Potential**:
  - o Rental prices can vary, but you can typically charge between $15 to $50 per day per item. High-quality, well-maintained gear can command higher rates, especially in popular tourist destinations.
  - o **Pro Tip**: Ensure all items are clean, safe, and in good condition to attract more customers and earn positive reviews.

- **Platforms to Use**:
  - o **BabyQuip**: A dedicated platform for renting baby gear to traveling families, allowing you to create a profile and list available items.
  - o **Rent Baby Gear**: Another marketplace focused on baby gear rentals, where you can connect with families in your area.
  - o **Facebook Marketplace**: A local choice for listing your baby gear, reaching travelers directly in your community.

- **Realistic Expectations**: Depending on your inventory and demand, you could earn between $200 to $1,000 per month. High-demand seasons, like summer and holidays, may yield higher earnings.

- **Getting Started**:
  - o **Choose a Rental Platform**: Sign up on BabyQuip or similar services.

- **List Your Items**: Create detailed listings with photos, descriptions, and rental prices.
- **Market Your Services**: Share your listings on social media or local travel forums to attract customers.
- **Ensure Quality and Safety**: Regularly inspect and keep your gear to ensure it meets safety standards.

66. BECOMING A DRIVER FOR FOOD DELIVERY OR PACKAGE DELIVERY SERVICES (E.G., DOORDASH, AMAZON FLEX)

Joining a food or package delivery service allows you to earn money by delivering meals, groceries, or packages in your area. This flexible work can fit around your schedule.

- **How It Works**: Drivers use a smartphone app to receive delivery requests. After accepting a job, they pick up the order from a restaurant or store and deliver it to the customer. Drivers typically earn money per delivery, plus tips.

- **Earnings Potential**:
  - Earnings can vary based on location, demand, and hours worked. On average, drivers can earn between $15 to $25 per hour, including tips. Some drivers report earning up to $1,000 per week, especially during peak hours or busy seasons.
  - **Pro Tip**: Maximize earnings by working during peak hours (lunch and dinner) and in high-demand areas.

- **Platforms to Use**:
  - **DoorDash**: A leading food delivery service, allowing drivers to work flexible hours and keep 100% of their tips.
  - **Uber Eats**: Another popular food delivery app, offering competitive pay and the opportunity to earn tips.
  - **Amazon Flex**: A package delivery service where drivers can earn money delivering Amazon packages, with flexible scheduling options.

- **Realistic Expectations**: Depending on your location and the number of hours you work, you could earn anywhere from $200 to $1,000 per week. Factors like tips and bonuses can significantly affect total earnings.

- **Getting Started**:

- **Sign Up on a Delivery Platform**: Create an account on DoorDash, Uber Eats, or Amazon Flex.
- **Complete Background Checks**: Most platforms require background checks and vehicle inspections.
- **Download the Driver App**: Use the app to receive delivery requests and track earnings.
- **Start Delivering**: Choose your hours and begin accepting delivery requests.

CHAPTER 8:
PASSIVE INCOME – EARN WITHOUT MUCH ACTIVE WORK

67. INVESTING WITH MICRO-INVESTING APPS LIKE ACORNS

Micro-investing apps allow you to start investing with minimal amounts of money, making it easier for beginners to build their portfolios.

- **How It Works**: Micro-investing apps round up your purchases to the nearest dollar and invest the spare change into diversified portfolios. For example, if you buy a coffee for $3.50, the app will round up to $4.00 and invest the extra $0.50.

- **Earnings Potential**:

  o Although micro-investing may not yield significant returns quickly, it can accumulate over time. The average return on a diversified investment portfolio ranges from 6% to 10% annually, depending on market conditions.

  o **Pro Tip**: Consistently using these apps can help you invest small amounts regularly, leading to substantial growth over the years.

- **Platforms to Use**:

  o **Acorns**: One of the most popular micro-investing apps, Acorns allows you to invest in spare change and offers various portfolio options based on your risk tolerance.

  o **Stash**: This app combines micro-investing with personal finance education, letting users invest in fractional shares of stocks and ETFs.

  o **Robinhood**: While primarily a trading platform, Robinhood allows users to invest with no commission fees and offers the option to buy fractional shares.

- **Realistic Expectations**: With consistent use, you might accumulate a few hundred dollars within the first year, which can grow to thousands over time, especially with compound interest. However, investing always carries risks, and there's no guarantee of returns.

- **Getting Started**:
    - **Download a Micro-Investing App**: Choose an app like Acorns or Stash and create an account.
    - **Link Your Bank Account**: Connect your bank account to ease transactions.
    - **Set Your Preferences**: Choose your investment goals, risk tolerance, and the type of portfolio you want.
    - **Start Investing**: Make purchases and let the app round up your spare change or make one-time deposits to grow your investments.

68. EARNING INTEREST WITH CRYPTOCURRENCY SAVINGS ACCOUNTS

Cryptocurrency savings accounts allow you to earn interest on your digital assets, often at higher rates than traditional savings accounts.

- **How It Works**: You deposit cryptocurrencies into a savings account offered by a cryptocurrency platform. The platform lends out your assets to borrowers and pays you interest for the use of your funds. Interest rates can vary widely based on market conditions and the specific cryptocurrency.

- **Earnings Potential**:
    - Interest rates on cryptocurrency savings accounts can range from 4% to 12% or more annually, depending on the asset and the platform. For example, Bitcoin savings accounts might offer lower rates than stable coin accounts, which are pegged to traditional currencies.
    - **Pro Tip**: Diversifying your deposits among different cryptocurrencies can help maximize your returns while managing risk.

- **Platforms to Use**:
    - **BlockFi**: Offers competitive interest rates on Bitcoin, Ethereum, and other cryptocurrencies, along with a user-friendly interface.
    - **Celsius Network**: Known for its high interest rates and no withdrawal fees, Celsius supports a wide range of cryptocurrencies.
    - **Nexo**: Provides interest on a variety of digital assets and offers a cryptocurrency credit card that lets you spend your crypto.

- **Realistic Expectations**: Depending on your deposits and the interest rates offered, you could earn a few hundred dollars in interest each year. However, the cryptocurrency market is volatile, and prices can fluctuate significantly.

- **Getting Started**:
    - **Choose a Cryptocurrency Platform**: Sign up with a reputable platform like BlockFi or Celsius Network.
    - **Create an Account**: Complete the registration process and undergo any necessary identity verification.
    - **Deposit Cryptocurrency**: Transfer your digital assets to your savings account.
    - **Earn Interest**: Check your account and enjoy the interest accrual over time.

69. OPENING A HIGH-YIELD SAVINGS ACCOUNT WITH CASHBACK OPTIONS

High-yield savings accounts (HYSA) provide a way to earn interest on your savings while some offer cashback rewards on purchases.

- **How It Works**: HYSAs offer higher interest rates than traditional savings accounts, allowing your money to grow faster. Some accounts also provide cashback on debit card purchases linked to the account, giving you a bonus for everyday spending.

- **Earnings Potential**:
    - Interest rates on HYSAs can range from 0.5% to 4% annually, depending on the bank and current market conditions.
    - Cashback rewards can range from 1% to 2% on eligible purchases, offering added earnings on your everyday spending.
    - **Pro Tip**: Use your debit card linked to the HYSA for regular purchases to maximize cashback earnings.

- **Platforms to Use**:
    - **Ally Bank**: Offers a competitive high-yield savings account with no monthly maintenance fees and a solid interest rate.
    - **Marcus by Goldman Sachs**: Known for its high-interest savings account and no fees, but it may not offer cashback options.

- o **Discover Bank**: Offers a high-yield savings account with cashback on qualifying purchases through their debit card.
- **Realistic Expectations**: Depending on your balance and spending habits, you might earn $50 to $200 in interest and cashback combined annually. The key is to keep a healthy balance in your account and use it for regular expenses.
- **Getting Started**:
  - o **Research High-Yield Savings Accounts**: Compare options based on interest rates and cashback offers.
  - o **Open an Account**: Sign up online and complete the required documentation.
  - o **Deposit Funds**: Transfer your savings into the high-yield account to start earning interest.
  - o **Utilize Cashback Offers**: Use your debit card linked to the HYSA for everyday purchases to earn cashback.

70. BUYING AND SELLING DOMAIN NAMES

The domain name market offers a unique opportunity to profit by buying and selling web addresses.

- **How It Works**: Domain flipping involves buying domain names at a lower price and reselling them at a higher price. The key is to find catchy, memorable, and potentially valuable domain names that businesses or individuals may want in the future.
- **Earnings Potential**:
  - o Some domain flippers have made thousands of dollars from a single domain sale. For example, the domain "Business.com" was sold for a whopping $345 million in 1999!
  - o **Pro Tip**: Look for trendy keywords or phrases or consider buying domains with popular extensions like .com, .net, or .org.
- **Platforms to Use**:
  - o **GoDaddy**: A well-known domain registrar where you can buy and sell domains. Their auction feature allows users to bid on premium domains.
  - o **Flippa**: A marketplace for buying and selling websites, including domains. Flippa allows you to list

your domains for sale and connect with potential buyers.
- o **Sedo**: This platform specializes in domain name sales and allows users to list their domains for sale and negotiate prices with buyers.

- **Realistic Expectations**: While some may earn substantial profits, others might struggle to sell domains. Setting a reasonable price and targeting the right audience is crucial.

- **Getting Started**:
  - o **Research Domain Names**: Use tools like Google Trends to find popular keywords or phrases.
  - o **Purchase Domains**: Register available domains through platforms like GoDaddy or Namecheap.
  - o **List for Sale**: Use marketplaces like Flippa or Sedo to sell your domains.
  - o **Market Your Domains**: Promote your listings on social media or through online ads to reach potential buyers.

71. STARTING A DROP-SHIPPING STORE

Drop-shipping allows you to run an online store without holding inventory, making it a low-risk business model.

- **How It Works**: In drop-shipping, you set up an online store and partner with suppliers who manage inventory and shipping. When a customer makes a purchase, you send the order to the supplier, who ships the product directly to the customer.

- **Earnings Potential**:
  - o The profit margin in drop-shipping typically ranges from 15% to 45%, depending on the products and suppliers you choose.
  - o Successful drop-shippers can make anywhere from a few hundred dollars to several thousand dollars monthly, depending on their marketing efforts and product selection.
  - o **Pro Tip**: Focus on niche products with less competition to maximize your chances of success.

- **Platforms to Use**:
  - o **Shopify**: One of the most popular platforms for creating drop-shipping stores, Shopify offers user-

friendly tools and integrations with various drop-shipping suppliers.
- **Oberlo**: A drop-shipping app that integrates with Shopify, allowing you to find and import products directly into your store from suppliers.
- **WooCommerce**: A WordPress plugin that enables you to create an online store and includes features for drop-shipping.

- **Realistic Expectations**: While the first setup may be straightforward, building a successful drop-shipping business requires consistent marketing and customer engagement. Expect to invest time and effort to see significant returns.

- **Getting Started**:
    - **Choose a Niche**: Research market trends to find a profitable niche.
    - **Set Up Your Store**: Create an online store using Shopify or WooCommerce.
    - **Find Suppliers**: Use Oberlo or similar platforms to source products for your store.
    - **Market Your Store**: Use social media, Google Ads, and influence partnerships to drive traffic to your store.

72. RENTING YOUR WI-FI HOTSPOT FOR MONEY

If you have a Wi-Fi hotspot, you can rent out your internet connection to others, offering a unique way to earn money.

- **How It Works**: Certain platforms allow you to share your internet connection and get paid for it. Users can rent your Wi-Fi hotspot when they need connectivity, particularly in areas with limited access.

- **Earnings Potential**:
    - Earnings can vary depending on demand and your location. You could earn anywhere from $20 to $100+ monthly by renting out your hotspot, especially in high-demand areas.
    - **Pro Tip**: Ensure your internet connection is dependable and has sufficient bandwidth to attract renters.

- **Platforms to Use**:

- o **Snomble**: An app that connects people looking for Wi-Fi with those willing to share their connection, allowing you to earn money for your hotspot.
- o **WiFi Map**: This app allows users to discover Wi-Fi hotspots in their area and connects them with those willing to rent out their connection.
- o **Fon**: A community-driven Wi-Fi sharing platform where users can share their internet connection with others and earn rewards.

- **Realistic Expectations**: While renting your Wi-Fi may not make you rich, it can provide a steady income stream, especially if you live in a tourist area or near schools and universities.

- **Getting Started**:
  - o **Sign Up on a Platform**: Choose a platform like Snomble or Fon and create an account.
  - o **Set Your Price**: Decide how much you want to charge for access to your Wi-Fi.
  - o **Promote Your Hotspot**: Share your Wi-Fi rental availability on social media or local community boards to attract renters.

73. AUTOMATING A PRINT-ON-DEMAND STORE FOR MERCHANDISE

A print-on-demand (POD) store allows you to sell custom-designed products without keeping inventory. This business model is ideal for those looking to enter the e-commerce space with minimal upfront investment.

- **How It Works**: Print-on-demand services enable you to create custom products like t-shirts, mugs, and phone cases. You upload your designs to a POD platform, and when a customer places an order, the product is printed and shipped directly to them. You only pay for the product after you've made a sale.

- **Earnings Potential**:
  - o The profit margins in print-on-demand can range from 20% to 50%, depending on your pricing strategy and the costs of production.
  - o Many successful POD entrepreneurs report making anywhere from a few hundred to several thousand dollars a month, especially during peak seasons like holidays.

- **Pro Tip**: Focus on niche markets or trending topics to increase the visibility and desirability of your products.

- **Platforms to Use**:
    - **Printful**: A popular POD service that integrates seamlessly with e-commerce platforms like Shopify and WooCommerce, offering a wide range of customizable products.
    - **TeeSpring** (now known as Spring): This platform allows you to create and sell custom apparel and merchandise, with an easy-to-use interface.
    - **Redbubble**: An online marketplace where artists can upload designs to be printed on various products. It manages production and shipping, allowing you to focus on design and marketing.

- **Realistic Expectations**: While setting up a print-on-demand store is relatively straightforward, successful marketing and consistent quality design are essential for attracting customers and generating sales.

- **Getting Started**:
    - **Choose Your Niche**: Research market trends to find a profitable niche or theme for your merchandise.
    - **Create Your Designs**: Use graphic design software (like Canva or Adobe Illustrator) to create eye-catching designs.
    - **Set Up Your Store**: Choose a platform like Shopify or Etsy to launch your store, integrating it with your chosen POD service.
    - **Automate Your Processes**: Use tools like Zapier to automate order processing and marketing tasks.
    - **Market Your Products**: Use social media advertising, influence partnerships, and SEO to drive traffic to your store.

74. RENTING YOUR VEHICLE'S ADVERTISING SPACE

If you have a car, you can monetize it by renting out advertising space on your vehicle. This method allows you to earn passive income simply by driving around town.

- **How It Works**: Companies pay you to place advertisements on your vehicle. You may have stickers, wraps, or decals featuring the company's branding, and you earn money based on how much you drive.

- **Earnings Potential**:
  - Vehicle advertising can earn you anywhere from $100 to $600 per month, depending on your location, driving habits, and the size of the ad.
  - **Pro Tip**: The more you drive, especially in high-traffic areas, the more you can earn.
- **Platforms to Use**:
  - **Wrapify**: This platform matches drivers with advertisers looking to promote their brand. You can earn money based on the miles you drive and the routes you take.
  - **Carvertise**: A company that pays drivers to advertise on their vehicles. You need to meet certain driving requirements, but the pay can be lucrative for regular commuters.
  - **StickerRide**: A mobile app that allows you to earn money by placing stickers on your car. You get paid for driving in designated areas and for the miles you cover.
- **Realistic Expectations**: While renting your vehicle's advertising space is a great way to earn passive income, it may not be a consistent or substantial source of income. Earnings can vary based on the demand for advertising in your area.
- **Getting Started**:
  - **Sign Up on a Platform**: Choose a platform like Wrapify or Carvertise and create an account.
  - **Provide Vehicle Details**: Enter your vehicle information, including make, model, and condition, and any preferences for the type of advertising.
  - **Get Your Vehicle Wrapped**: If selected, the company will arrange to wrap your vehicle with their advertisements, often at no cost to you.
  - **Drive and Earn**: Start driving, and earn money based on your driving habits and the terms agreed upon with the advertising company.

75. BUYING FRACTIONAL SHARES IN RENTAL PROPERTIES

Investing in rental properties has traditionally needed substantial capital, but with the advent of fractional ownership, you can now invest in real estate without needing to buy an entire property.

- **How It Works**: Fractional ownership allows multiple investors to buy shares in a property. This means you can own a percentage of a rental property and receive a proportional share of the rental income and potential appreciation in value.

- **Earnings Potential**:
    - The returns on real estate investments can vary widely but often range from 8% to 12% annually, depending on market conditions and property management.
    - Investors can also receive help from property appreciation, which can lead to significant profits over time.

- **Platforms to Use**:
    - **Fundrise**: This platform allows you to invest in real estate through a variety of offerings, including residential and commercial properties. You can start with as little as $500, making it accessible to many investors.
    - **Roofstock**: Roofstock focuses on single-family rental homes. You can buy fractional shares in these properties or invest in a whole property. They provide detailed analysis and cash flow projections.
    - **RealtyMogul**: This platform offers a range of real estate investment options, including REITs and direct investments in rental properties. They have a low minimum investment threshold, often starting at around $1,000.

- **Realistic Expectations**: While investing in fractional shares of rental properties can provide attractive returns, it is important to understand that real estate investments come with risks, including market volatility and potential tenant issues.

- **Getting Started**:
    - **Research Platforms**: Explore different real estate investment platforms to find one that aligns with your investment goals and risk tolerance.
    - **Create an Account**: Sign up for your chosen platform and complete any required verification processes.
    - **Choose Your Investment**: Browse available properties and select the ones you want to invest in based on your budget and desired returns.

- o **Make Your Investment**: Buy fractional shares and track your investment performance through the platform.

76. PEER-TO-PEER CAR RENTAL (E.G., HYRECAR FOR UBER DRIVERS)

With the rise of the gig economy, peer-to-peer car rental services allow you to rent your vehicle to others when you're not using it, generating extra income effortlessly.

- **How It Works**: Peer-to-peer car rental platforms connect car owners with people looking to rent vehicles. You can list your car for rent, set your price, and choose the rental period. Renters can book your car directly through the platform.

- **Earnings Potential**:
  - o Rental income can vary depending on your vehicle type, demand in your area, and how often you rent it out. Many car owners earn between $30 to $100 per day.
  - o For those renting to gig workers (like Uber or Lyft drivers), the demand can be consistent, potentially generating several hundred dollars monthly.

- **Platforms to Use**:
  - o **Turo**: One of the most popular peer-to-peer car rental platforms, Turo allows you to list your vehicle, manage bookings, and set pricing. You can earn money renting your car out, and Turo provides insurance coverage for rentals.
  - o **Getaround**: This platform enables you to rent your car hourly or daily. Getaround also offers a feature that allows renters to unlock your car using their smartphone, simplifying the rental process.
  - o **HyreCar**: Specifically tailored for rideshare drivers, HyreCar allows you to rent your vehicle to Uber and Lyft drivers. It's a great option if you're looking to earn money while your car is idle.

- **Realistic Expectations**: Renting your car can be profitable, but it requires upkeep and insurance considerations. You need to keep your vehicle in good condition, and there may be periods when your car is not rented.

- **Getting Started**:

- **Choose a Platform**: Select a peer-to-peer car rental service that meets your needs and sign up for an account.
- **List Your Vehicle**: Provide details about your car, including make, model, year, and any unique features. Upload high-quality photos and set your rental price.
- **Set Rental Guidelines**: Decide your availability, rental terms, and any specific requirements for renters.
- **Manage Bookings**: Once your car is listed, check incoming rental requests, communicate with renters, and make bookings through the platform.

CONCLUSION

Congratulations on completing *Clicks to Cash: 76 Ways to Make Money Online with No Real Skill*! You've now explored a diverse array of methods that can help you earn money online, ranging from the straightforward to the creative, and everything in between. The possibilities are virtually limitless, and the opportunities are at your fingertips.

Embrace Your Potential

In a world where technology has transformed the way we work and live, the potential for making money online has never been more accessible. Whether you're looking for a side hustle, aiming to pay off debt, or seeking a path toward financial independence, you have the tools and knowledge to take action. Remember, the journey to financial freedom often starts with a single step. Don't be afraid to experiment with different methods to find what resonates with you.

Stay Committed and Adaptable

One of the key takeaways from this book is the importance of commitment and adaptability. The online landscape is constantly changing, and what works today might not work tomorrow. Stay curious, be willing to learn, and keep adapting your strategies to stay ahead of the curve. Follow industry trends, engage with online communities, and continually refine your skills. By staying informed and flexible, you'll be better equipped to seize new opportunities as they arise.

Set Realistic Goals

As you embark on your journey, set clear and achievable goals. Whether you want to earn a few extra dollars each month or replace your full-time income, having specific aims will help keep you motivated and focused. Break your goals down into smaller milestones and celebrate your achievements along the way.

Build a Support Network

Consider joining online forums, social media groups, or local meetups focused on your chosen methods of earning money. Surrounding yourself with like-minded individuals can offer valuable insights, encouragement, and accountability. Sharing your experiences and learning from others will not only enhance your knowledge but can also make the process more enjoyable.

Act Today

Now is the time to put your newfound knowledge into action. Choose a few methods from the book that resonate with you, conduct further research, and start experimenting. Whether you decide to set up a print-on-demand store, take part in paid focus groups, or invest in fractional real estate, the first step is always the hardest. But remember, every expert was once a beginner and taking that first step is crucial.

Final Thoughts

As you embark on your journey to making money online, remember that success is not solely defined by the amount of money you earn. It's about the skills you develop, the experiences you gain, and the financial freedom you achieve. Embrace the learning process, and don't be discouraged by setbacks. Each challenge is an opportunity to gain experience and improve.

Thank you for taking this journey with me. I hope you find success and fulfillment in your online endeavors. Here's to your future of earning, learning, and thriving in the digital age!

www.ingramcontent.com/pod-product-compliance
Lightning Source LLC
Chambersburg PA
CBHW070114230526
45472CB00004B/1258